ENTRY FROM B[...]

BINOO K. JOHN is a senior journalist based in New Delhi. He has worked with several media houses, including the India Today group and *Indian Express*. He is the founder and director of the Kovalam Literary Festival and owns the bookselling portal Makemeread.com. *Entry from Backside Only: Hazaar Fundas of Indian-English* was first published in 2007 and became an instant bestseller. His other books include the critically acclaimed *Under a Cloud: Life in Cherrapunji, the Wettest Place on Earth* (2004), *Curry Coast: Travels in Malabar 500 Years after Vasco Da Gama* (1999) and the novel *The Last Song of Savio de Souza* (2011).

Praise for Binoo K. John's books

'With a journalist's flair for combining information with easy readability, John provides sharp, cheeky insights into the early flowering of the language...'

—Manjula Padmanabhan in *Outlook*
on *Entry from Backside Only*

'Lovely, witty, acutely observed book with some marvellous descriptions of places and people.'

—Alexander Frater, author of *Chasing the Monsoon*,
on *Under a Cloud: Life in Cherrapunji,
the Wettest Place on Earth*

'*Under a Cloud* is one of the finest pieces of Indian travel writing ever.'

—Ravi Shankar in *India Today*

ENTRY FROM BACKSIDE ONLY

HAZAAR FUNDAS OF INDIAN-ENGLISH

BINOO K. JOHN

RUPA

Published by
Rupa Publications India Pvt. Ltd 2013
7/16, Ansari Road, Daryaganj
New Delhi 110002

Sales centres:
Allahabad Bengaluru Chennai
Hyderabad Jaipur Kathmandu
Kolkata Mumbai

First published by Penguin Books India 2007.

ISBN: 978-81-291-2377-0

10 9 8 7 6 5 4 3 2 1

The moral right of the author has been asserted.

Typeset in AGaramond Pro 11/14 by Jojy Philip, New Delhi.

Printed at Thomson Press India Ltd, Faridabad

Dedicated to

my uncle, the late C. J. Cherian (1905-1995),
icon of his time, adored teacher of English, among the first
recipients of the President's Medal for teachers;

my father, the late K. C. John (1924-2005),
journalist for half a century;

and my mother, the late Aleyamma John (1925-2009),
who sat me down to teach me English and maths.

CONTENTS

FOREWORD TO THE NEW EDITION

India's love-hate relationship with English is fascinating to study. When I made the attempt to chronicle some of the Indian 'quiddities', as Nigel Hankin, the author of *Hanklyn-Janklyn*, says, it was a leap into the dark. Aimed at a non-academic readership, the intentions were humble: that *Entry from Backside Only* would get published, and it would be read by a few thousand people. The first edition published by Penguin sold about 12,000 copies, taking both author and publisher by surprise. Now Rupa is trying to give this book a second wind with this new edition.

Clearly there is an abiding interest in language, its usage and its evolution. This book looks at the written word and how we have been using English: by twisting and turning grammar, vocabulary and phraseology to serve our smaller clerical purposes as well as our aspirational ones. Indians have held on to English for dear life. At various phases during post-independence history, there were efforts to reinforce the use of Hindi and, soon enough, there were counter-movements in favour of English. The constant use of English by Gandhi and Nehru actually formed the basis of the Indian love for writing in English, though not necessarily for speaking in English.

There are various estimates about the number of people in India who actively use English. The point of interest, however, is that English is sought to be used by the aspiring classes of nearly 30 crores of people. They are the twisters and turners of the language and have given the language a new phraseology, which we call Indian-English and which we scoff at. What we don't often realize is that patois is a way a language evolves and English, being a global language, has been enriched by its assimilation into and osmotic pull-ups from other languages.

Indian-English has now gained a life of its own. It is irreverent, inimical to ideas of purists, frames its own rules, gives its own meaning to English words and, after sprouting from the streets, ensconces itself in the big books of bureaucratese, newspapers, self-published books—and from there into the Oxford dictionary.

Like the Caribbean mongrel English, Indian-English too is set to have a life of its own: fifty years down the line a fully Indianized English, with its lavish spread of Tamil, Malayalam and Hindi words, will rule the roost. It may have an umbilical cord to the mother language, but its existence will be bereft of its puritanical supervision. In other words, India would have appropriated English for its own use. To the puritans, the middle finger.

In the half-decade since the first edition was published, I have noticed that the usages of Indian-English pointed out have continued their relentless march forward, occupying space in newspapers and classifieds and so on. I have not tried to add many more examples of such usages and have satisfied myself with the fact that the language is taking the road I predicted. It is simply time to accept Indian-English and to stop ridiculing it. That is how language grows.

A typical example is the title of this book: 'Entry from Backside'. It is easy to scoff at and there are many funny examples of its usage. But who is to understand that? Backside is a favourite usage in Indian officialdom and in the streets and has even made its way into Hindi. Everywhere, from the remotest corner of Uttar Pradesh to the upscale promenades of New Delhi, 'Aap *backside* se jayiye' is accepted usage. Indian-English has had a backside entry into the world of mongrel languages. And there it will sprout and from there branch out.

This second edition I hope will be received with much *halla gulla* and will not result in this tired author getting a kick in his you know where.

New Delhi   Binoo K. John
October 2012

THE WRITING ON THE WALL

Carry out your own bag
Avoid to use polythene bag
— Admonition at the entrance of a
Mother Dairy booth in Delhi

Among various missions that a Delhiite carries out in a day, this one would be the toughest. It consists of 'carrying' your bag with you as you go 'out' of your house to buy vegetables at the Mother Dairy outlet. While the bag helps you carry out your task, how, we wonder, do we carry out the bag as well?

Indian-English has found easy sustenance and publicity in government-sponsored hoardings, brochures and flyers, in textbooks and bazaar guides, in letters to the editor… The first and most obvious facet of this great Indian patois is the inability to differentiate between literal and idiomatic or metaphorical usage. When the literal encroaches on the metaphorical, strange Siamese twins are born, joined at the intestines—with two brains, ganglias all wired up in separate ways, though the genetic template is the same. Though they get succour from the same source, they are often petulant and individualistic and figure out their own figures of speech.

Indian-English survives beyond any logic. Its terrain is an over-ploughed one, its IQ straitjacketed between the primary and the geeky, its memory galactic and capable of summoning words from centuries past, its survival instinct similar to that of the chameleon, changing colours in different locales: Hinglish here, Tamglish there.

Even death has given occasion to the spread of Indian-English, as I was to see during a trip to the innards of Tamil Nadu. Near a village was a series of five shops, two of which announced a new industry: post-mortem freezing. While we are all quite familiar with 'almost freezing to death' in winter, here you can be 'freezen after death'. In these shops, where aluminum boxes with embedded compressors are stacked up, you can 'prolonge your mortal remains as lengthy as possible'.

In India, as everywhere, English offers its own problems. It becomes a language of 'iffs and butts' where double 'f's and double 't's crop up at the most unlikely of places, giving emphasis where there should be subtlety. The problem is compounded by the fact that many Indian languages are onomatopoeic and English is not strictly so. Worse, Indian languages dispense with the definite article. The tea-shop owner who tried to augment his menu by introducing egg-based dishes can be pardoned for offering 'Home Late' for that terribly common everyday dish made with egg and slices of onion and tomato. To expect the tea-stall owner to keep track of the 'e's and 'm's in omelette would have been a bit too much. He obviously must have imagined this as the two-minute dish one prepares when reaching home late. Purveyors of pure English can go to hell and spelling sticklers can chew their blue pencils.

Enough labels and tags have not been invented to describe the variations of English that are sprouting across the country. Linguistic misuse does not seem to worry the users of such bastardized forms of English but it has gained its own constituency and acceptance. There's Hinglish, there's Malglish and Tamglish, all of which have their own peculiar ways of embellishing words and adding value to meanings. 'The Indian gift of knowing what words mean' is what James Cameron, author of *Indian Summer*, calls this phenomenon.

So India is a cacophony of English from the farthest village to the mega malls of glitzy megapolises. It is a language that has evolved and drifted down from the higher echelons of government offices where the bureaucracy starts all its letters with 'Whereas' and job applications end with the promise that 'if given the job I will enhance my performance to the best of my abilities and strengths, god willing'. It is the English that has crept up unchallenged from the streets, where shopkeepers and hoarding painters send out messages to all humanity—like this tea-shop owner in Cuddalore in Tamil Nadu: 'One minute relax, one-day happy'. Or this telephone booth operator opposite Dal Lake in embattled Srinagar who has put up a notice as a measure of caution to the user about the unpredictability of his digital meter: 'Meter jump to be paid by the customer'. Adroit covering of business risk, apparently.

The enhancement of performance is a nationally felt need. It is the war cry of all the sexologists who operate in the bylanes of Indian cities. To them should be given the honour of propagating Indian-English in the teeming gullies and mohallas of the Hindi heartland and giving it that hilarious edge absent in the otherwise drab English of suburbia. Hastily written plates and boards atop lamp-posts (another Indian-English usage) and bigger hoardings tucked away near the halwai's shop in the old (Brit or Mughal) parts of north Indian cities offer panaceas for 'secret diseases'. There are solutions offered for 'nightly emission' and 'maximum satisfaction guaranteed for nightly activity' and ayurvedic tablets for 'big hard of the organ' which will then go on to give 'intensified pleasings to partner and happiness in marriage'.

The problem of confronting and adopting or mastering the English language has been with India (yeah, other countries as well) for over four centuries, and still continues. A hybrid form of English or Hinglish stalks the land and is not only accepted but quite popular. Use of a few English words like 'tension' and 'ready' in an otherwise Hindi conversation shows the connect with the larger world, or at least smacks of some level of ambition and erudition. Though Indians prefer to speak in one of the about thirty languages that are their mother tongues, most documents are written in English, even in remote villages, which makes necessity the mother of invention, giving rise to a hybrid form of the written language. When it comes to the hand that writes, there is a sense of apprehension about the usage, but the document comes out in English nevertheless. When it comes to putting pen to paper, or paint-brush to hoardings, Hindi is discarded for what is seen as a higher form of communication, as we shall discover in this romp through Indian-English.

Caught between the inability to articulate in a foreign language and the rather inexplicable need to be seen using English, the average Indian gets the shivers. Over the years, with mobile phones and computers spreading all over India, the country's fascination with English has only intensified. It cannot be said for sure if this has resulted in English usage getting more communicative. At the moment the process is a bit haphazard and finding a method in this madness is the idea of this book.

The British over the years have pondered over the problem and in typical fashion tried to codify Indian-English usages to bring in some thematic coherence and also to solve the etymological riddles hidden in many Indian-English words. Henry Yule, one of the co-authors of *Hobson-Jobson,* the Indian-English dictionary, talked of 'Oriental words highly assimilated perhaps by vulgar lips to the English vernacular'. The glossary was one of the early efforts (first published 1882) to make sense of the linguistic tamasha. 'The words which we have to do taking the most extensive view of the field are in fact organic remains deposited under the various currents of external influence that have washed the shores of India during twenty centuries and more', Yule and his co-author A. C. Burnell wrote.

About twenty-five years after the *Hobson-Jobson* effort, civil servant George Clifford Whitworth also put together an Anglo-India dictionary. Not stopping at that, he decided to teach Indians the right grammatical usages by pointing out Indianisms. In 1907, he wrote *Indian-English: An Examination of the Errors of Idiom made by Indians in Writing English* (Garden City Press). Though he did not talk down to Indian users of English, he was clearly perturbed by the way English was going berserk in the hands (and mouths) of Indians.

I hope no one will take up this little book expecting to find an amusing collection of those linguistic flights to which imaginative Indians occasionally commit themselves. I am myself too painfully conscious of the immense superiority of Indians to Englishmen in the way of acquiring foreign languages for the preparation of any such work to be congenial task to me. No, my purpose is entirely different and is perfectly serious. For many years past, both in hearing arguments from the Bar and in reading Indian books and newspapers, I have been struck with the wonderful command which Indians—and not only those who have been to England—have obtained over the English language for all practical purposes. At the same time, I have often felt what a pity it is that men exhibiting this splendid faculty should now and then mar their composition by little errors of idiom which jar upon the ears of the native Englishmen.

In the introduction to the book, Whitworth writes:

> Considering in conjunction with this great natural ability that the Indians are the inheritors of the most elaborate language that the world has known and that their forefathers regarded grammar *(vyakaran)* as a *vedanga* or limb of their sacred Veda, it seems well worthwhile to try and render them a small service by showing them how their admirable knowledge of our language may be made still more complete.

The effort to gently or forcefully improve the language is an ongoing one. Indian-English has been the subject of much mirth and amusement, especially when used in bestselling novels by Indian writers, at least two of which became classics in the last century: *All About H. Hatterr* and *The Inscrutable Americans*.

Sticklers might guffaw, but if Indian-English finds more space in everyday conversation it is because people like the small-town professor managed to break through the idiomatic and metaphorical complications of English and went straight to the heart of the matter.

English words and pronunciations continue to flummox us, so do spellings. Of course, the disconnect between pronunciation and spelling is a universal problem, so it cannot be pinned down as an Indian characteristic.

Newspaper cliches are what keeps Indian-English growing, stacking up words by the day, squeezing out non-existent meanings, dragging in reluctant Hindi words to serve as the morning's laugh-inducing headline and in the process sending the purist scurrying for cover. What does an Englishman straight arrived from London make of this heading: 'FM *maange* more'? or 'Phirang brokers asked to keep off commexes' (*Economic Times*, 4 May 2005)? Well, in the first place, these headings are not addressed to the purists, they are targeted at the large number of people who have Hindi as their primary language but borrow heavily and frequently from English to buttress their language and also as a password to elite gatherings.

The Hindiization of English thus stands in direct opposition to the Coca-Colanization of regional languages, which are parallel streams. The sheer number of people who speak Hindi has in a sense stood as a bulwark against the spread of 'pure English' or Queen's English, if at all there is something like that. Hindi has instead liberally injected its own usages and peculiar charms into English, making Indian-English quite a popular form of communication. Like fast-spreading weeds, Hindi and other Indian languages have swarmed the original form of English. Words which were Indian-English contributions have found a prominent place in standard English dictionaries. With their rising influence in the complex world of computer programming, Indians are bound to influence the language more and send out 'Indian viruses' which, over the years—as we have seen—have the ability to worm their way into the heart of English and corrugate its smooth exterior.

The philological dimension of Indian-English has thus been an enduring concern.

It is not easy to gauge whether it is Hindi words which are getting into English or whether the cross-border infiltration is 'vice-versa', to reuse a word favoured by Indians. Either way, it has helped the spread of the language. It is not just English that extends its borders to take in new allies but Hindi and other Indian languages too have easily adopted English usages and words both in common usage and in the written form. Which is why the taxi driver at the airport will tell you that 'Yeh route mein jam hoga'. Two English words in an uttered cluster of five is the national average.

Bollywood, of course, has done its bit in extending the scope of Indian-English. It has over the years spoofed Indian-English usage and in the process added new vocabularies which have easily segued into everyday usage. 'Mera bad luck hi kharab hai' (my bad luck is bad) is one that mocks the urchin-turned-hero who mouths it. Bollywood is not just the supplier of entertainment, it is the benchmark of social trends, fashion trends, upheavals in hemlines, plunges in stock markets and necklines, and the originator of an entire genre of Bollywood argot and Ajit (a criminal mafia don archetype complete with moll Mona and sidekick Rawbert) jokes, pegged mostly on bilingual puns.

In the Shah Rukh Khan blockbuster *Main Hoon Na*, there is this classic instance of a spoof of Indian-English. In the school compound, a flirty Hindi teacher accosts the hero with the favourite Indian opening word, 'myself'. Normally it is 'myself in-charge here', or 'myself an engineer', 'myself own this harvest land' and 'myself do all the culture here', a typical misuse of agriculture. So this teacher too adopted the same opener: 'Myself Hindi teacher. You meet me in the backside when my period is empty.'

Backsides have a frontal position in Indian-English. In cluttered, crowded alleys, there can be seen the notice 'Entry from backside,' a usage not exactly meant as a come-hither line to gays. In India, backsides are not just entered, they are beautified too. However, when there is 'backside beautification in progress', entry is banned. People often remember backsides so well that they promise or are cautioned to 'use the backside only'. With the battering that backsides are put through in India by frequent entries, it is a surprise that front entries are used at all.

But the word Indian-English itself is open to various interpretations. Books by Indians in English, especially fiction, are referred to as Indian-English writing, or the more arch usage, Indo-Anglian writing. My friend, expat novelist, professor and critic, Tabish Khair, in his high-sounding critique called *Alienation in Contemporary Indian-English Novels* (OUP) uses the term Indian-English to refer to all Indian writing in English. In this book, the term Indian-English is hyphenated and used in a more pejorative sense to refer to English as it is spoken or written by all Indians, not just authors. Of course, this is all relative since it will be difficult to point out which is the all-correct standard English and who are the people who use it.

But does Indian-English exist or is it an urban construct aimed at pulling down the aspiring populace? Is the label a ploy by the arriviste to shunt out the surging crowd at the Pearl Gates of linguistic Utopia? Does it exist outside the imagination of the privileged class as a 'used language' with form, shape, a tangible ambition and an unwritten constitution, driven by the acquisitive mania of an emerging nouveau-Anglo class?

There is a surging crowd, of course, at the marketplace of Indian-English. Every Sunday morning, the streets of New Delhi's Daryaganj overflow with English books brown with age and disuse, tattered by being carried around and offered for sale from gunnybags by the kilo. Here, books do indeed have weight, and disproportionate gravitas as well. The Sunday book market converts the big town crassness and filth of the narrow street connecting the Doric-pillared and concrete-tiered New Delhi with the Mughal Old Delhi into a street cocking a snook at the idyllic Hay-on-Wye book market. The setting is kitschy and messy. The sidewalk houses chatwallahs who place their wares on a bamboo tripod, the old Golcha cinema which has a ghostly aura despite the film posters and further ahead the lip-smackingly famous Moti Mahal restaurant, the inventor of the universally acclaimed butter chicken, which also makes the best chicken tikkas and kakori kababs. As you walk along, the thought strikes you that on the street just turning off to the left is Karim's restaurant which has the barra kababs and the melt-in-the-mouth seekhs fit for kings.

Here, they come from all parts of the country to buy cheap books in English, the Hindi-to-English dictionaries written by the legions of English professors, the photocopied engineering and medical books and, of course, Shakespearean tragedies ('special expert notes on Hamlet for all degrees'). On weekdays, the road is an ugly picture of all that has gone wrong with Indian cities. On a lucky Sunday, from the pile of books that glut yesterday's dirty footpath will crop up an antique book, a first edition or a book owned by a British officer, which the seller will fling at you for a hundred rupees, thrilled that he has got rid of 500 grams of the 10 kilos of books he hopes to sell that day. Though Hindi and other regional books are also on sale, it is the English book—dog-eared novels, shrink-wrapped pirated 'Oxford dictionaries', old English magazines—that the crowd is after.

Many of them are first buyers of English books, so the ten or twenty rupees that a tattered English book costs in Daryaganj is a safe investment. A few young boys were looking at the *Amit Students Compact Dictionary (Hindi to English to Hindi)* which cost ₹100, published by the Students Book Depot, Nai Sadak, in the innards of Old Delhi.

Every few feet there is a section for ₹10 books, where the seller will be shouting *'Dus rupaiya, dus rupaiya,* imported novel', just like his counterpart on Janpath, a few kilometres towards the south, would sell men's briefs and 'lady panty' with a rhythmic bass *'Do ka dus, do ka dus'* (two for ten). The hollering here in the 'imported novel' section of the footpath stops only to dismiss an onlooker who wants two novels for ₹10. Lying by the side there, unsought and doomed, next to the tattered shoe of the shouting salesman is *Politics of a Rational Left* by Eric Hobswan. That must wait for some professorial eye.

I picked up the *History of English,* what else, for ₹10. The bookman turned it around as if examining if the glue of the binding still held and then extended it to me saying *'pachees'* (twenty-five) before settling for a more moderate valuation. He had the demeanour of a merchant banker while assessing the value of the book. The Daryaganj market is also a front for many pirated books and for the huge numbers of guides and textbooks for the various degrees that are manufactured in the nearby Nai Sadak, which is the unlikely centre of Indian publishing in English if just volume is the criterion.

Indians, like other users of English around the world, have hiccups with punctuation marks, more so the apostrophe. While the comma does not come within the purview of the average Indian writer of the English hoarding, the apostrophe is very much there, hanging in the air. The popular hang-out for that crescent-shaped mischief-maker is outside government offices and restaurants, bristling with advice and moral stipulations.

'Our motto: Citizen's First' says the sign outside a Delhi police station. The common understanding is that the apostrophe prepares you for what is to follow: the plural 's'. In that sense, it is also a farewell to the singular form. It is also subliminally believed in India that the apostrophe hanging between the singular and plural forms is a unifying factor, a hand-holder between two types of words.

If at all geography can be linked to punctuation marks, then Goa, where the most people in India use spoken English in their daily lives, could take the top prize. Every restaurant in Goa offers 'lobster's', like the one I had for dinner in Candolim on a rain-drenched night. When the power went off and I was alone and lost, I sat there counting the misplaced apostrophes as if I was on a grammatical mission.

In Goa, people were not told to 'Carry out your own bag' but were offered 'bag's'. 'Buy two bag's. Get one free', said a board in a nearby shop trying an English pitch to pump up its low monsoon sales. In fact, I had entered the restaurant because 'all rare fishe's' were on offer. As I walked back in the dark, raindrops falling on my raincoat-cum-windcheater—the same orange-hooded Gap I had worn when I went to Cherrapunji in 2002 to write on the rains there—sounded like drumbeats from the devil's lair. It was a scary night, but I loved the rains and I was alone and free and had only some misplaced apostrophe's (oh how could I get this one wrong?) to spot.

But soon enough, along Candolim's dark eerie road that day, with the rain beating strange rhythms on the raincoat, there was the Dim Dong restaurant, which you could visit for 'Punjabi Dishe's', but there was a bigger sign nearby saying 'Closed'. The shutters had come down on the world around me, and being June, the clouds had opened up.

If, in the written form, the apostrophe and the 's' are used when not required, in the spoken form, words ending in 's' are often deprived of the letter. But while the letter may be missing, the spirit never flags. 'Everyone know English here. I learn from school', Silvio Fernando, the taxi driver in Goa told me. Young Goans' interest in and adoption of English comes from their constant interaction with foreigners, theirs being a tourist economy. Historically, of course, there was the influence of the Portuguese and then the British.

Come to think of it, there is no reason why people in Goa or anywhere in India should speak English the way it is prescribed by others who claim correct English to be their own. But a matter of interest here is how geographically too English has taken on various forms. The spoken form is, however, of interest, considering the local variations.

Day number two in Goa was peaceful, with the sky painted blue as if to make up for the grim grey of the previous day. As I stood near the grounded and rusting ship *River Princess,* which gave the beach of Candolim an eerie touch, I chatted up the lone fisherman Joaquim who was trying to take advantage of the waves to catch some catfish.

'This ship has been lying for four years. A Japanese ship also got grounded over there. They came cut it up and afterward took it away. Here it has been four years with this Goan ship and nothing has been done. Now the contract has been given to a British company.'

The next day while I was talking to another fisherman, Manuel Rodrigues, I discovered another way of dropping the 's'.

He had been waiting for a tug on his line for a long time when I went to him. Raindrops were falling and the sea was churning in anticipation, the waves lashing the coast throwing up enough spray to wet us.

'Yesterday I play with sting ray for one hour. I gave it a long line. Kept pulling. I play with it again. It is risky, you don't know what *happen.'*

This book hopes to capture the new grammar and the vocabulary, the essence, the unintended humour, and the way Indian-English has sallied forth in the country despite a national guilt about using English. In this endeavour, which I have done to the 'best of my abilities' as the Indian prayer in job applications ends, I hope I will achieve what I set out to. I 'humbly' offer this book to the Indian 'peoples' in the hope that at least 'under standing people will not suffer'.

2

THE WRITING ON THE BOARD

Since the first publication of this book in 2007, an entirely new class of people who use Indian-English has emerged. They are the virtual warriors—those who comment on articles which appear on news and current affairs portals. They only comment on the Internet and are an abrasive, aggressive breed of writers, mostly Indians settled abroad who frequently write back home. Many such comments on discussion boards are instant and easy interventions in national debates. Such messages are mostly meant as a reassertion of nationalistic credentials, which the writers feel have been diluted since they left the shores of their motherland and hence, in a way, betrayed the country of their birth.

These are not people who would print out a letter and send it to the newspaper by snail mail. Nor have they possibly written letters to the editor while they were in India. They totally skipped the snail-mail era and would not be able to remember the last time they posted a letter. Aspiration is predominant in their minds. A sense of nostalgia, tinged with guilt, drives their correspondence. The majority pick articles by commenting on which they can reassert their love of the motherland. Needless to say, they are mostly right-wingers who espouse an intolerance that they probably did not feel when they were settled in India. There are fine commentators as well, but the space is crudely overrun by the virtual warriors. If one follows the correspondence, one can figure out that the astute commentator often leaves the discussion board, exasperated by the number of uncouth messages.

Almost always common to these virtual warriors is the fact that they are new entrants to English writing or correspondence and hence use Indian-English: they have little option since replying in an Indian language is not possible and would not serve the larger purpose of being part of a national debate. But the Roman script is frequently used for transcribing Hindi abuse. Unlike other theories projected elsewhere in this book, the language used by most such writers has unique qualities. Apart from being rabid, the authors make no effort at being seen as users of correct English. For them, 'correct' English usage is actually a hindrance to the expression of their views. And so they invent their own versions of language. Impatience too is a hallmark and their rants are not given the benefit of a spell-check. These users of Indian-English cannot differentiate between wrong and correct usage, and if confronted with their sentences betray no remorse.

What makes these people write and, in most cases, write back to India? One plausible explanation is that discussion boards are easily accessible and comments can be posted instantly—the writer achieves a sense of self-gratification since he has struck a blow for the cause that he espouses. Also, real names, addresses and IDs can be hidden, unlike in typed or emailed letters to newspapers. The interactive nature of the board is exciting because various such commentators end up brawling until it flares into a full-scale verbal conflagration and the administrators close down correspondence. Beside rumour mongering, false propaganda and fresh airings of favourite popular myths are always crucial attractions.

I tracked articles on Gujarat to figure out why right-wingers get so agitated over any news reportage from that state. I also tracked responses to my own articles on nationhood and nationalism that I wrote through 2012 on Firstpost.com. In response to any article in which I supported any Congress move, I was branded an agent of the Pope or of Sonia Gandhi, both of them being seen as Christian and foreigners and thus equals in their dislike of India. A majority of these did not use the word Muslim and always referred to members of the community as 'skullcaps' or 'lungi-clad'.

Here is a typical rant from Rediff.com (an ability to distort fact or whitewash history is a characteristic of such writers):

> Gujarat Brothers and Sisters, beware of rigged EVMs that the only way Congies can win as they did in 2004 and 2009. The Congies have fallen to such lows that to retain power they will do anything..

And again:

> Bloody Kangress Rabid dog posing as IAC activist. Why are u denying that Muslims are not compatible with freedom and democracy because of sharia.

Giving grammar and syntax the go-by, here is a goodbye message to Bal Thackeray, who died on 17 November 2012.

> The Lion the only saffron leader whom I liked is Balaji!! Balaji I will miss you very much. Mumbai will miss you. The end

of an era Balaji's body consigned to flames .Wish you hv a wonderful journey in the Heaven [here, note the imagery of death as a journey to heaven]. Lakhs of ppl hates him but I think he was real patriot not fake like Advani!!

To an article in which I said that the cricket league IPL is now a global brand that Indians should be proud of, Saurabh Aj commented:

> I think writer is poor guy who now had money and he is more powerful that world. His references like sita, salt, moral, black money means he doesn't know India expect ipl.

For every article, there are a couple of people who rise to the defence of an imagined Hindu India bereft or cleansed of minorities and the lower castes. This can include any reference to Indian mythology. In my case, I am dismissed as a member of a minority who has no right to comment on India. According to Prasanpd:

> You are a bugger bloody! When you say Sita as icon is in imagined India what do mean she is in realistic India. I wonder how come you are still not booted out!

Amazingly, many readers never object to the use of Indian-English, though they react as soon as any communal issue is raised or the India of their imagination is tarnished with the brush of robust logic. The popular historian Ramchandra Guha calls them the 'intensely chauvinist tribe of Internet Hindus'. The reason is letters like this, which follow the pattern stated above, quoted in his book *Patriots and Partisans* (Penguin):

> After British left India all British invaders left India, why Muslim invaders were not evicted? What right Nehru and

> Gandhi had right to keep tens of millions of Muslims after giving them 'homeland' [read 'Hindu land']?

And:

> India is bound 2 be worldpower. Take my words. People like Mr Guha are agents of China and they also go to temple (though in the dark of night)?

Another reason for the new-age letter writer to rave and rant on the computer is because it provides them the scope of writing in any way they want. Spellings can be contorted (like '2 be') or invented (like 'who will vote 4 Kangress?'); numericals can exist side-by-side with alphabets (perhaps pardonable in the Twitter age); and whenever conventional spelling fails them, they can always resort to their own version ('doble-do-gook', for instance).

The pet hatred is of course Sonia Gandhi; any mention of her name in a positive light is attacked immediately. Very often, Sonia is referred to by her Italian surname, which all these writers remember but none have bothered to remember spellings of even commonly used English words. Note that when English sentences fail them, they quickly change to Hindi and produce composite bilingual sentences—a phenomenon that is fast gaining popularity and acceptance in the country. Nearly fifty writers commented on my article which suggested that the triumphalistic hanging of Kasab may be sign of a Congress sway to the right as an electoral ploy ('Is the Congress leaning right with Kasab's hanging?', Firspost.com, 22 November 2012). One of the commentators said:

> Become slave of sonia Gandhi and prosper in life.. My My what a powerful woman, all giant political leaders serve, why can't I

Saurabh Goswami on a Rediff.com discussion board:

> Sonia is an imported Italian glue. Throe her and her party out.

And Sudhir Sood wrote:

> With the close up photos she is looking like a female DEVIL

Viki Raghuvanshi joined the debate, using all the above-mentioned devices of nonsensical spelling with this direct attack at the author (in this case, myself):

> nation suffers bcz of disgraceful Hindu-hater sikular like this bloke. What did US do to Osama entered Pak shot him and buried him in sea. Lets C if he has guts to rant on tht.

Such message writers are mostly male and often use imagery commonly used by the Indian male. Rarely though it happens, women too join these discussion boards. Note the generous use of exclamation marks by Rashmi, which is a characteristic of Indian-English users as explained elsewhere too:

> really don't understand what rubbish article and the quality of authors, FP publish !!! hanging a terrorist is right-shift… !!!common you sick-lair people.. you don't miss a chance to bark your sick mindset !!!!

Notice that the number of exclamation marks grows with the rising anger of the writer. Also, targeted words such as 'secular' are deliberately misspelt or punned on. Says Ghoda:

> Scamgress is all the way "right" but is pretending to be sickular! Now it has proven to be wrong &will be send in to oblivion!

This is from Arun Kumar Mitra:

> Maybe this was the main master plan in the mind of UPA
> chair person Sonia Manio. President Pranab who turned
> down the pleas of Kasab so soon was also the faithful servant
> minister under Sonia Madam's and Rahulji's ministry.

Now the switch hit, to borrow a cricket phrase.

> Kasab gaya accha huya. UPA sarkar ka gameplan kya hai isme
> is the main question??

Mahatma Gandhi, always suspect in the eye of the extreme
right, is also dragged into such Internet debates. Various theories
are propounded. One particular commentator has named himself
4thAugust1932 and goes on to inform us about the significance
of this date:

> To promote Gandhi/Nehru hegemony in India, bania Gandhi
> betrayed Independent Nation for Muslim/Christians/Anglo-
> Indians/Sikh/SC/ST people in 4th August 1932 Round Table
> Conference.

This is yet another instance of how an imagined India cleansed
of all minorities and lower castes remains the ultimate dream of
the Hindutva proponent. An interview with economist Bibek
Debroy by the redoubtable Sheela Bhatt on Rediff.com evinced
this comment. After warning readers of 'Congress paid workers
in discussion board', Jena Bharati writes:

> They are pure jihadis allaghirs from porkMHS and they will
> "negate India and its achievements

Again note that, like in the case of 'secular', the word

'Congress' is also frequently punned on and a derogatory word is produced. Mostly it is 'Con'.

> spreading canard won't help con-gress much in K'taka election.
> In any case Con will be decimated.

In a way, it is encouraging to see that the discussion board has encouraged people, so far outside the realm of the English writer, into barging into that rather rarefied world and staking their claim to the language—and also to the larger national debate that is a corollary.

3

HERE A QUACK, THERE A QUACK

Classifieds written so fluently in broken English

B.O (Body Odour)
May come to you if you are careless!
—Life Buoy advertisement, 1938

India's dalliance with English began when the East India Company arrived in India in 1608. It became a marriage of two incompatible partners through the centuries of the Raj. The fascination for English gathered tremendous momentum— ironically enough—after the British left. This strengthening could be a nostalgic harking back to the Raj or it could have been the urge to better what the colonial regime left behind.

Either way, English steadily grew on India. The best evidence of how the language became the favoured mode of written communication can be seen in the journals of the eighteenth century. When it came to an important communication, it had to be in English. This was because of the early start that English journalism had and also because advertising in English papers was seen as prestigious. The language also helped the message reach the English and the elite class, who were in any case the target audience, having the required purchasing power. So intense was this desire to communicate in English that some of the earliest newspapers and journals in India were in English or bilingual.

Of course, like everything else, this linking up can also be traced to the Minutes of 1835 which, as critic Jason Boldbridge argues in a paper on Indian-English, officially endorsed Thomas Babington Macaulay's civilizing mission of forming 'a class who may be interpreters between us and the millions whom we govern—a class of persons, Indian in blood and colour but English in taste, in opinion, in words and in intellect'.

Much of what Babington Macaulay said in the Minutes had the power of prescience:

> The problem in India is that we have to educate a people who cannot at present be educated by means of their mother tongue. We must teach them some foreign language. The claims of our own language it is hardly necessary to recapitulate. It stands pre-eminent even among the languages of the West. It abounds with works of imagination not inferior to the noblest which Greece had bequeathed to us; with models of every species of eloquence; with historical compositions...with just and lively representations of human life and human nature... Whoever knows that language has ready access to all the vast intellectual wealth which all the wisest nations of the world created. English is likely to become the language of commerce throughout the seas of the East...Whether we look at the intrinsic value of our literature or at the particular situation of (India), we shall see the strongest reason to think that, of all

foreign tongues, the English tongue is that which would be the most useful to our native subjects.

Much before this near-prophetic statement, as Sajni Kripalani Mukherji points out in an essay on The Hindu College (*The Illustrated History of Indian Literature in English*, Permanent Black), Philip Francis had written in a letter to Lord North:

> If the English language could be introduced into the transaction of business...it would be attended with convenience and advantage to Government and no distress or disadvantage to the natives. To qualify themselves for employment, they would be obliged to study English instead of Persian. If schools were established in the districts...a few years would produce a set of young men qualified for business, whose example and success would spread and graft the institution gradually into the manners of the people.

As we know, there was a 'central design', as Mukherji says, in enforcing the use of English and speedily sidelining the vernacular and Persian. This happened quite fast and the fact that traders too took to English—not exactly like a duck takes to water, but rather more clumsily, as we shall see—helped in the entrenchment of Indian-English. It is still growing, promising to become a language far removed from the original, and far more accessible to the Indian population than the correct English over which the elite claims proprietary rights.

From the early days of the Raj, fervent efforts were made to make English compatible with India and Indian languages. Throughout British rule, many writers addressed this problem— like Clifford Whitworth, whose attitude was sympathetic— and offered many theories for some element of compatibility. Edward Farley Oaten, BA, LLB, 'late scholar of the Sidney

Sussex College, Cambridge', prefaced his *European Travellers in India,* published in 1909, thus:

> A few remarks are necessary on the subject of the orthography of Indian names. In quotations the original (Indian) spelling has been followed, whether it be the crude 'Jno.Gernaet' of the 17th century travelers or the diacritical exactness of the Indian Text series. In the other parts of the essay I have not thought it worthwhile to adopt an elaborate system, but have aimed at simplicity, at the same time shunning uncouth forms and avoiding inconsistencies as far as possible. That I have not entirely succeeded in my main or subsidiary aims, I am fully aware.
>
> … In closing I wish to acknowledge my indebtedness to numerous editors and authors of works of recent date… A work on such a subject as that of the present essay would demand the labour of years, rather than that of months and could be attempted by no one who was not a master of at least nine or ten entirely different languages…

But without a yearning on the part of Indians to take to things British, the imposition of English would not have been possible. Such display of admiration and a sort of servile attitude to the British was clearly evident in the first Indian editorial in English which appeared in the *Bombay Samachar* of 1 July 1822:

> Be it known that in India before the establishment of British rule there have been great Hindu kings and mighty Mogul monarchs and governors. During their rule there have been eminent Sankritists, Persian and Arabic scholars, as well as other savants deeply versed in the then known great sciences and numerous are the books and many are the instructive tales compiled and told by those great scholars and savants, which are still extant and which are being seen and read by us

now. But after the institution of British rule in India, when the efficiency and wisdom, science, art, and knowledge and justice and splendour of the British manifested themselves, and we began to understand a little what real popular happiness was, it became clear to us that the magnificent brilliance of their learning and knowledge has eclipsed those great learned Indians of former times. The old administration was at the evening twilight, whereas British rule and every achievement connected with it shine and blaze like the sun. Before the predominance of the British in India when either the Hindus or Mahomedans were at the helm of Indian government, all state affairs political, military, literary, judicial and mercantile were transacted in secret and managed under the rose, [nose, I guess is what the writer meant] thus virtually precluding the people at large from knowing how they were governed and what happened about them. But in the present British administration all matters touching either the ruler or the ruled are allowed to be published daily in newspapers for the benefit of the subjects. In former times no one dared even to dream of such a liberty. British authors themselves openly acknowledged in several books that the affairs of their countrymen were formerly administered with the same arbitrary secretiveness and that in times gone by they were also ignorant and foolish but by dint of assiduous efforts they gradually improved and that through the agency of the printing machine the publication of hundreds of thousands of copies of the same valuable books having been facilitated, science and art and national life came within range of public knowledge...

No wonder the world resounds with their fame...and it is by now reasonably believed that their invention of the printing press will stand us in good stead...be it known that in every territory under the British flag newspapers printed in the English language have become a permanent institution...

Nothing unusual in all this. The role of the English press in India was going to be as crucial over the years as it is now. It was not just dissemination of information that the English press did. It drew in large numbers of people to practise the language. Some thrust the language with greatness, some attained greatness using the language, others plodded along with the genre called Indian-English.

The complexities of communicating to an Indian audience, Anglo-Indian audience or purely English audience were many. Advertisers of Indian products resorted to their own version of the English language and journals of the last three centuries present us with sterling examples. The tradition of various Indian goods, mostly cosmetic and health products, being advertised in Indian-English begun in the eighteenth century lasts till today. Such classified and display advertisements form an entire genre of Indian-English that has withstood the ravages of time and tide and offered classic examples of Himalayan blunders.

A particular trendsetting advertisement generated the phraseology for years to follow, and the terms it used graduated to common use. A parallel stream of localized English usage was thus established which came to be accepted and obviously propagated. Advertisements in many English papers even today reflect the early struggles with the language seen in the classifieds of the eighteenth century, and show how little has changed, though the borders of the language have shifted tectonically during this time. There has been a heavy tilt towards appropriation of local usage, regional metaphor and patterns of speech. As we shall see, the sheer contempt for correct usage and the domination of the trite were essential ingredients of Indian-English.

The most amusing Indian-English appears in ads issued by quacks—who had the biggest adspend of the nineteenth and the early part of the twentieth century. Some medicines were imports from England and typically promised 'easing pain when taken internally' with 'healing virtues when applied externally', like the Daviss Pain-Killer did in the 2 January 1876 issue of *The Bengal Times* published from Dhaka. This painkiller positioned itself as a purely vegetable compound. 'It is eminently a family medicine', and like all medicines offered a cure-all package. 'It is not only a good remedy for Bruises, Cuts, Burns etc, but also for Dysentry or Cholera or every sort of bowel complaint.'

On 22 January of the same year, Halloway Pills espoused the cause of the healthy man and offered cures ranging from killing pain to eliminating liver and kidney disorders. Indian-English was the argot of all these ads.

> This medicine has resisted every test which time, prejudice and vested interest could impose upon it, and it at length stands forth triumphant as the most reliable remedy for those derangements of the system so common as the change of seasons. When the air grows cooler and the functions of the skin are retarded, an occasional dose of Halloway's Pills will call on the liver and the kidneys for great activity and compensate the system for diminished cutaneous action. As alternatives, aspierient [aspirate: draw (fluid) by suction from a bodily vessel or cavity] and tonics these pills have no equal. To every aged and delicate person whose appetite is defective, digestion infirm and tone of health low, this medicine will be a precious boon, conferring ease and strength.

Phew! Such pitches made mostly in single- or double-column spreads seemed to have served their purpose, for Halloway Pills was a consistent advertiser through the last part of the nineteenth century and the early years of the next.

By the twentieth century, many such tonics were also sold as cosmetic products, and language was the very powerful delivery system. The *Bombay Chronicle* of January 1921 has this insertion about 'The God-sent versus Ordinary Amritdhara or Vital Drops'. The ad made claims which were in keeping with the tone, grammar and vocabulary of the Indian-English ads of the period.

> Over 24 thousand unsolicited testimonials…Amritdhara is the one-in-all remedy. It cures itself all chronic diseases… In one Word, Diseases Disapper, Pains Vanish, Hopes Revives, Life Comes Again

By 1948, such 'one-in-all remedy' ads had not only gained in popularity but had also invented new idioms and usages and become cocky enough to offer rewards of 500 pounds as the Octogen (herbal tonic) had done, 'to any scientist or Medical Man or any of the public who proves the inefficiency of our most wonderful invention'. Like today, aphrodisiacs were peddled as cure-all remedies.

Prepared by Parke Davis, which has since gone on to better things, Octogen promised:

> … surprising increase in vitality and energy within the first 24 hours. It makes a man or woman look and feel 15 to 20 years younger than the actual age. It is useful for loss of vigour, weak memory and body nervousness, impure blood, sickly skin, depression, insomnia, giddiness mental or physical exhaustion. It will increase your height from 2 to 4 inches and your weight will he increased from 5 to 10 lbs…

If all that was on offer was not enough, Octogen summoned poetic phrases to buttress its positioning.

> The Roses return to your cheeks and your appearance is improved 100 per cent. The brilliance and lustre on your face will be the same.

Competing with imported English oils were Indian variants which resorted to the same strategy of the Kolkata-based pharma companies; the *Debar Herald* (sometimes also called *Bihar Herald*) published weekly from Bankipur was the carrier of many such ads including this one by Surama Oils, which used the Q&A format in the 5 July 1913 issue:

> WHAT IT IS? Surama is a highly scented and spotless hair-oil which possess the special virtue of preserving and enriching the hair
>
> WHAT IT IS FOR? It is for the use of the fashionable ladies and gentleman of society who always look for a high class hair oil for hath and dressing.
>
> How TO USE IT? Use it daily at your morning bath or evening toilet. Apply it and wash off your head with cold water. When you have dizziness, vertigo and a heated brain use as directed.

While quacks survived everywhere, even after 'washing off your head' to get rid of the 'heated brain', what is intriguing is why they advertised so regularly in English papers when they could make do with regional papers, and why even their hoardings or nameplates gloried in English words. Such efforts did not have the guidance of the English script writer, since quacks were confident of their own vocabulary. The answer lies of course in their search for some sort of credibility and class, which an English brochure or an English noticeboard gave them. The Surama oil ad thus unambiguously offers it to 'fashionable ladies and gentlemen of society who always look for a high-class hair oil'. Inserts in regional papers would not have reached 'fashionable ladies and gentlemen'. To position a product at the high end of the market required the backing of the English language.

Many products were linked to royal usage, an easy strategy to position the product as a premium brand, and English advertisement was part of the packaging. C. K. Sen & Co. Ltd did exactly that with Jabakusum oil, calling it The Royal Toilet and labelling it 'By appointment to the Princess of India'. The ad went on to claim that 'it is used by Maharajas and Maharanis of India'. Not to be left behind, Kaviraj N. N. Sen advertised his Keshranjan oil as 'prepared under princely patronage', and 'the only high-class Indian Hair oil'. Sen exhorted the readers of the *Herald* to 'use Keshranjan To Day and decide for yourself which you will use hereafter'.

The unending search for 'high-class' and 'fashionable ladies and gentlemen' brought a larger audience into the ambit of English usage. So there was this impatience to learn to use English—or often, plunge into English usage without so much as a by-your-leave.

On page 5 of the same issue of Bankipur's *Bebar Herald* is the ad for The Healing Balm. 'A single dose is effective/Radical cure in a week' it announced. The rest of its high-falutin claim was rather characteristically put within brackets:

(removes nervous weakness, giddiness of the brain, loss of appetite, constipation, pain in the back and abdomen loss of sight and hearing, mental and bodily prostration, muscular and local weakness)

And in keeping with tradition and the search for credibility, there is a footnote claiming that 'Healing Balm is approved, endorsed and supported by highest men of medical profession'. The makers of Healing Balm also issued warnings against other brands, where their Indian-English was tested to the maximum.

Imitation: On all sides—Beware and insist on having the Genuine thing. There are 'Balms' and 'healers' on all sides and do not waste money for a trash.

In the 5 July issue, a manufacturer of one of these oils makes his appearance in name—no wonder, since the product carried his name. 'K.D. Sircar's Non-Mercurial Pills' used mystique, pseudo-science and some impressive English words to push his product. Mercury was his targeted enemy. Mr Sircar then reveals the magic of his creation:

I received its recipe from a Muhammadan fauqir in the Nepal Jungle, towards the end of the Indian Mutiny. It is free from all sorts of mercury. It has hitherto been distributed gratis but its increasing demand, consequent, on its spread of its reputation for wonderful curative process, and consideration of delicacy & prevent further gratuitous distribution. Infants and children suffering from hereditary diseases, as well as women during gestation are not excepted; the latter cured by external application only (internal use being strictly prohibited during pregnancy).

Such insertions often ended up preaching the opposite of what they meant. Which is why Octogen's 'It is useful for loss of vigour' should actually be understood as 'prevent loss of vigour' and 'the brilliance and lustre on your face' is not supposed to remain the same. Words were given meanings they did not legitimately carry, like Sircar's 'gestation'. Phrases were also used sometimes with meanings difficult for you and me to decipher, but comprehensible to the target readership, as in this advert by Lahiri & Co, Chemist, Druggist, Booksellers, Bankipur, who regularly advertised 'SpecTcles'. 'Just opened spectacles department [notice the second spelling of spectacles after the botched attempt in the heading]. Get our quotation before you purchase from anywhere else; it will pay you [which probably meant "you will gain from it"].'

Whether Lahiri's challenge to check out competitors' prices paid off or not is difficult to figure out. But the advertisements definitely paid handsomely. Otherwise quacks with imported products would not have taken the trouble to make their presence felt in classifieds. Like the mysterious seller of 'Electric solution', which was the 'sensational discovery of America'. The solution 'ends or concentrated Electric Current the want or superfluity of which in the human constitution causes all sorts of diseases. It acts like a charm where Allopathic, Homeopathic, Hakimi or ayurvedic medicines totally failed'.

This search for a 'higher' language continues throughout the history of the Indian encounter with English starting with the 'Macaulay mission' and going on through various stages of education, administrative reforms and then reaching up to that elusive search for an elitist social status. An advertisement in English announced quite a lot apart from the product itself. In many cases, it is the name of the advertisers which is sought to be projected.

Quacks did not have a monopoly on broken English and other segments of users too had a whale of a time with English. Products which are today household names started out with quite modest targets and rather modest taglines, like Life Buoy, which now has a multi-crore advertising budget and is an important product in the stable of FMCG giant Hindustan Lever. When it started out, Life Buoy ads could not be distinguished from many other efforts of traders and individual salesmen.

The February 1939 issue of *Bombay Chronicle* had this special insert for the soap which has over the years positioned itself as a product for macho men wallowing in dirt. When it started out it had an olfactory objective: to do away with body odour.

Life Buoy
Don't Risk IT!

[Before jumping to the conclusion that this was an advertisement asking the readers to avoid buying Life Buoy, read below!]

B.O (Body-Odour)
May come to you—if you are careless!
    Body-Odour results in loss of friends and happiness. And it is in crowded places that 'B.O' is most noticeable.
    It's impossible to stop perspiring. Perspiration is natural and healthy; but when its left to clog the pores of the skin it soon becomes stale and leads to offensive Body-Odour!

If many such ads left behind a stink, it wasn't noticed. What mattered was that the ad had to be in English. Trying to forge a connect with English was an effort that could be seen at every level. A girl student of the Institute of Home Economics was quoted in the BBC book *The Story of English* as saying: 'Every guy wants his wife to know English so that she can move about with him in society. If you go to parties and clubs you'll be more attracted towards a person who's talking in English rather than Hindi'. The student has put her finger on the pulse of Indian society. In such a society, to spread English was a cake-walk.

Astrologers also often took the cue from quacks and advertised their services in Indian-English, the complexity of their craft compounded by the way they groped around for the right meanings in English and often and inexorably ended up using totally misplaced phrases, misspelt words, and metaphors. Indian-English owes not a little to this unseen band of hoarding painters and advertisers who over the years have been champions of Hinglish.

The late Henri Cartier-Bresson, during his perambulations through the country to capture the pains of Partition, shot a picture of a roadside astrologer in Mumbai in 1947 who had advertised his services thus: 'Great Care of all Sarts of Diseases without medicine or troubles or pains which may be ailing you. If you are over come-d by jadu or Bhoot, palit. If you are out of Emp-loyment or Business go Slack & Not sho-wing any profit. Children do not live your heart…'

This astrologer, who looks straight into Cartier-Bresson's lens, like hundreds of his countrymen, was resorting to English to resolve a credibility problem, since the use of English, he felt, would give the impression that he was not just a Hindi heartland sadhu trying to make a living but one with the wherewithal to use the language of the sahibs. That would have meant high-class clients as well as those needing exorcism or magic mantras.

The sadhu would obviously not have targeted his skills at foreign tourists or the British in India alone. It was after all a subliminal urge among Indians to resort to English if they had any wares to offer. Since the huge noticeboard at the side of his shop does not use any Hindi words, it can be assumed that the astrologer with his powers to gaze into the future could well have seen that the writing on the wall would all be English. Confusion about spellings, which had dogged Indians from the day the Battle of Plassey was fought and lost, can be found in this board as well. 'Children do not live your heart' might possibly have meant to convey the fact that with a little help from this astrologer children would remain obedient and close to the parents.

He, like many other advertisers, felt that the use of English threw a ring of credibility around him.

The problem of credibility of the product was indeed severe and so many astrologers advertised in Indian-English just to defend their trade and lash out at 'charlatans' of the craft who dared take up prophecy as a career. The *Madras Standard*, one of the early English journals to be started by an Indian, had this spirited defence of 'scientific astrology'. It starts off with a quote from Dequincy: 'Astrology may be true but astrologers are consummate humbugs'.

Then starts an elaborate defence of astrology and an attack on others who claim to be astrologers in the 12 July 1895 issue. And, in keeping with a pattern, this attack on quacks was mounted by one of the tribe itself.

> The ancient Jyotishastra of the Hindus have been often brought into disrepute by mountebanks and Charlatans who seek to please everybody by prophesying future prosperity. The undersigned does not care to indulge in vague generalities of predictions and he can offer only truth and not flattery. His method is one of calculations according to approved systems and his terms are moderate. He invites a trial.

Having introduced himself as anti-quack, this Bangalore astrologer and 'lost horoscope maker' goes on to lay out the charms of his science in the type of Indian-English which lasts till today:

> Accurate answers to the following questions are given, number of issues, time of marriage, number of wives, length of life, obtaining employment, making adoption, acquiring landed estate, result of pending cases, fortune in mercantile cases, date of promotion, sincerety in partners and lovers.

By the next paragraph it becomes evident why M. Tholosalinga

Mudaliyar listed each of these contemporary problems rather elaborately, of which 'number of issues' rates higher than 'length of life' and 'sincerety in partners'. 'A fee of Rs 5 will be charged for a single question. Each application should invariably be supplemented with an advance of two rupees.'

The tradition of such advertising continues, which makes it easy for us to surmise that those who used Indian-English were not even looking for the correct form of English to address their audience. Correctness, or quality consciousness, has never been a national trait and so random usage, creative Hindiization, utter disregard for truth, have all been easily accepted. If Tholosalinga Mudaliyar adopted his version of English to convey his message, so did this spam email which landed in my inbox, as if with astrological precision, as I was writing this chapter. Considering that this astrologer also claims to be an information technology specialist (in keeping with fantastic claims that quacks always make, as we have seen) no wonder he took the spam route.

Sri Sai Jyotish Seva Kendra
Dear Sir

Today the life has became very fast and tough. Everyone is rushing behind the success and money and everyone wish to reach the first at the top, some of them get the success but unfortunately some get failure. Even after being succeed in professional or career front sometimes or luck stands against us and at the domestic front we found lot of struggles. We, a team of young learned professionals from IT and some other sectors gathered here for research on Vedic Astrology since past couple of years and with Aim and object to provide proper solutions to all the people suffering hard luck and struggling with different problems.

Some of us or our close nearest or dearest might be facing different problems either regular married life or problem in getting to married, after getting married delay in getting kids is another big issue. Jobs, business or health are another major front which can disturb our domestic harmony.

Our research is proven and we have found very excellent results in solving these kinds of problems and we have seen satisfactory results in after giving Vedic remedies. **These all predictions and solutions are free of any charge except detailed analysis reports and business problems. You have to just revert to our email address sai_jyotish@yahoo.com with your specific question with birth data (Date of birth, Time and Place) along with some past date of event to reconfirm the birth chart. Please mention one question at one time only.**

In order to make this program popular we wish that you will forward this email to all your friends and relatives to get maximum benefits.

Business problems, detailed analysis reports and Live chat with the experts for 15 Min. are available on payment of Rs.251/- only, which will be spend over the development of this program and social causes. Please ask us for Bank A/c name and number to deposit this money.
Sri Sai Jyotish Seva Kendra

From the ₹5 that Mudaliyar charged per question over a century ago, ₹251 for a fifteen-minute chat seems reasonable, though 'one question at one time only' remains a hitch. All along, sentence by sentence, we can make out how Indian-English has in fact defied any attempt at change. The only progress that can be detected is that Sri Sai Jyotish Seva Kendra has facilities like electronic transfer of money. And while Mudaliyar offered solutions to the eternal Indian problem of 'number of issues' (which to an astrologer can only refer to the number of children), Sri Sai Jyotish Seva Kendra brought back the real meaning of the word by suggesting that 'after marrying, delay in getting kids is another big issue'. A better catchline for Mudaliyar would have been 'Your issue, my creation'!

The hectoring tone of many such ads seems to be a time-honoured practice. The *Madras Standard* had Little's Oriental Balm announcing its 'cure-all' properties. 'DON'T BE BLIND' screamed the heading and then went on:

> Don't refuse to believe in a thing, till you've tried it. Thousands of people suffer the indescribable tortures of rheumatism because they have never heard of LITTLE'S ORiENTAL BALM or because they are blind to their own interest and refuse to try it.

And then comes the bottomline.

> There is no reason why any one should suffer with rheumatism if they have Re 1 to pay for a bottle of this unfailing remedy.

By asking customers to 'don't refuse to believe in a thing, till you've tried it', a deadly double negative, what the advertiser might have hoped for is exactly the opposite, that is, the customer must try out a thing and then repose faith in it. Such totally unintended meanings are a trademark of Indian-English usage, as we saw in the early part of this chapter.

Unfailing remedies were also targeted at the hair, not just the 'internals' and 'externals' of the body. Among the cosmetic ads of the nineteenth century, this one which appeared in the *Madras Standard* of 15 July 1895 is really hair-raising.

> Koko for the Hair
> Most positively stop hair from falling out.

But what about falling out with grammarians? Such ads might make the hair of sticklers stand up, but it should be noted that the users of Indian-English were least bothered about the niceties. There was a supreme confidence in the way Indian-English was used.

And in the same issue there was another cream seller offering his wares:

> MAKES the old young!
> The young younger!
> The cream always rise to the top and Baron's 'Nerve Recuperator' still holds its own as a non-pareil tonic food physically and mentally as well as in possession a power over diseases hither to unknown in Medical Science
> Price Rs 3 per bottle
> We still smile though competition is keen
> Baron and Co. chemists Broadway

Such advertisers always rose to the occasion, even though they did not necessarily 'rise to the top' as Baron's cream manufacturers claimed. Attacking competing directors, terming all aspirant cream sellers as quacks, they kept alive the first pages of the early newspapers by their claims and counter-claims. 'Beware of Cheap trash' often caught the eye of the reader. Ayurveds mocked at science frequently, like Austin and Co. from Broadway in Chennai: 'Try all science and non-science and then come to us for a permanent wonderful cure.'

It is not possible to ignore the role of these home remedy ads in the subliminal growth of Indian-English over the last two centuries. It is in such advertising launched ambitiously by private individuals and small companies and in modern days by the government that the misuse of English was propagated, survived and still flourishes.

If hair creams and Octogen cure-all remedies paraded their wares and prided themselves on the capturing and remodelling of an alien language for their own use, aphrodisiacs could not be far behind. This again from the *Madras Standard* in 1895: Pilula Poentia had a lengthy explanation considering the nature of the product and language was indeed a problem, more so because 'sex' was considered an f-word those days.

> Is not a quack medicine but pronounced by the leading member of 'healing art' to be a sovereign remedy for nervous debility, premature decay of Vitality loss of manhood. It also purifies the blood, revives the drooping and languishing spirit of the despondent, impart tone and vigour to the weak frame. A week's trial will work out miracles in the most obstinate and given off cases. Correspondence strictly confidential.

Pilula Poentia can be said to have admirably got over the problem of communicating sexual inertia by using the euphemism 'drooping and languishing spirit of the despondent'.

One hundred and ten years after Pilula Poentia announced its presence in the market comes Vigoura Hy Power, Nervine tonic for men. Nothing much had changed in the unabashed use of Indian-English, though the word sex is present in the heading itself. So, unlike in the Pilula case, there would not be any confusion in the reader's mind—at least initially.

Boost to Great Sex Drive

Vigoura Hy Power is a power-packed nervine tonic which has proved to be a magic potion for men between 18 and 70 years of age. With the use of this powerful aphrodisiac, man feels high-voltage sexual passion, culminating in fantastic pleasure. In fact this powerful formula of Vigoura Hy Power not only cures the symptom, but also supply redemptive energy to all the systems in the body. To top it all, it is the antidote for killing all the sex-related hazards. Apart from these, it is also a powerful potion to get rid of senility induced due to diabetes...

Apart from the not-too-subtle use of Vigoura, daringly remade from Viagra—and that too for a drug that offers itself as a 'patent homeopathic drug'—it is important to note that the imagery comes closer to the real thing when compared to the 'drooping and languishing' of the earlier ad. The 'high-voltage sexual passion culminating in fantastic pleasure' is as close as it can come in any form of Indian-English. The picture accompanying the ad of course has a white woman and man indulging in foreplay, but the 'shake well before use' that the package advises is obviously open to interpretation.

Such advertisements were quite significant considering the volume of literature they produced as reaction from readers and counter-advertisements from new traders trying to enter the market with a 'high-class' product.

In this sense, Hicky's contribution is noteworthy. Though as a Brit his English should have been correct, he opened up various avenues for the spread of English in the form of spoofs, slanderous pieces and long letters in defence of his art against government efforts to suppress it. All this drew a large number of other writers into the debate, giving Britishers and Indian users of the language big ideas and a mighty forum in his short-lived newspaper. In his paper we can see the first use of Hindi words by a Brit. After *Hicky's Gazette,* launched on 29 January 1780, no less than twenty-seven journals were launched in India in the next twenty years. It was a momentous period in the growth of the language in India. It was a flying start to Indian journalism.

Most important is the spoof Hicky used on quacks and medical practitioners. He was listed as both surgeon and apothecary in the records (journalism was clearly an afterthought) and so Hicky knew what he was talking about. Such spoofs took liberties with the language which later correspondents were to pick up.

A few lines are being quoted here to illustrate how much ads, articles, letters and spoofs on quackery dominated early Indian journalism. Hicky often summoned Hindi words for special effect, in the manner of Indian-English users today. He referred to one of his many rivals as 'Peter Nimmuck', giving him a salty flavour. Hicky's first journalistic reaction was to slander and to go for the solar plexus straightaway. That he chose quacks among his early victims should not be surprising.

> Such doctors who never say Leydon or Flanders,
> Run counters to reason, and bleed in the jaundice.
> If your wife has a headache let Sangrado but touch her
> And he'll job in his Launcet live any Log Butcher
> Tho' in putrid complaints, dissolution is rapid.
> He'll bleed you to render the serum more rapid
> But consider the cause sure, 'twill give one of the ship
> Man, To see dubb'd a doctor, a special good midshipman,
> Who handles your pulse as he'd hand a rope.
> And conceives your complaint, just as clear as the Pope...

Hicky also used prose to take another swipe at quacks, though his biographer S. Thankappan Nair, Kolkata's barefoot historian, believes that the following passage was Hicky's parody on his rival paper *India Gazette* (referred to as *Monitor* in the spoof). Be that as it may, all these spoofs and epistles were a big help in the formulation of early Indian-English writings, in giving people an idea of how to write and, more importantly, in shaping the content of Indian journals:

I Phaeton Lounger esq, an Assistant in the Secretary office, from taking too large a Dose of a medicine newly Introduced into Bengal, call'd the Monitor, prescribed by Doctors M...K and R...d, was immediately seized with an involuntary Stupor and universal *Lethargic Numbness of the senses, Pains in the upper region of the neck, Dizziness in the Pericranium,* and an intolerable weight on the Eyelids—A pinch of Strong Ruppee-Snuff it was thought would revive me—but it had not the desired effect. The further disagreeable Symptoms brought on by taking This Dose of Doct. R...d's Monitor were an excrutiating Colic—Gripping in the Abdomen, and a most horrible Senesmus. Being much alarmed, I sent for Doctor Kill-cranny one of the most Eminent of the Calcutta Faculty, who formerly out a Midshipman in the Rumbold Indiaman...Doctor Kill-Cranny pronounced my Case to be the Bile with a gentle schirrus in my liver.... he accordingly sentenced me to be rubb'd all over with mercury as if I was to be Tar'd and Feathered, making me swallow at the same time three Wash balls, which he said would lubricate the passages and carry off the Bile...After undergoing a variety of Bleedings, Blisterings Scarifications—Rowellings and tepid Emersions I found myself rather worse than better and verily believe that Doctor Kill-Cranny (tho' a very great physician) mistook my case for the Farcy.

In this deplorable state, a Brother Writer Rigdum Spouter Esq; of Lyons now prevailed on me to try only a single Dose of the pleasant prescription, prepar'd by Doctor Hicky, call'd Pills to purge melancholy, or the Enlivening Elixer of MIRTH, published and sold by the said Doctor Hicky at the same price as James Fever powders, in papers at a singly half Crown each. The very first Dose gave me instant relief, brought away the wind and occasioned an Astonishing Explotion. My spirits became light and jovial. The gloom occasioned by the Dose I had taken of the *Monitor,* was dispersed and by continuing Doctor HICKY's Extraordinary Medicine only 3 Weeks I find myself quite another Man... The Lethargic stupper has left me and the Abdominal gripings are totally removed. The only inconvenience I feel is a little remains of the Tenesmus, which I understand is now the general complaint and unavoidable symptoms attendant on all those who are patients, and happen to swallow even so small a quantity of that Narcotic, costive composition Doctor R...ds Monitor...

Hicky laid the foundation—now we know it was a firm foundation—for the growth of English journalism in any form. The spoofs and the rabid letters, the claims and counter-claims, the libel threats, the sweeping critique, the declarations of freedom, all written in English, inadvertently also helped the growth of the parallel form of English and also, as we shall see, even dragged in Englishmen to reluctantly use Hindi and other Indianized words.

If advertisements are the first resort of the Indian-English practitioner, brochures and other such manuals are also favourite platforms. A minuscule one-inch-by-one-inch pamphlet which I found inside a lock and key packet has these 'using instructions'. The instructions could have been avoided had the key not had a number lock facility. But the technology of the number lock had the manufacturer in a bind.

The cipher is set as '000' in the factory and you can remain it or setup yourself cipher as the following steps:

1. Push the adjusting sheath in the direction of the arrow and hold it, then turn the number to which you have selected, push the button as the direction of arrow and let the adjusting sheath pop-up and return to normal place.

2. Now the new cipher of your own have be set.

3. Turning the cipher to chaos direction is to a lock state.
4. Turning the number to which you have set and you will unlock it.

If this sounds like an excerpt from a *Cosmopolitan* article on how to find the G-spot, or the New Age guide to the Kamasutra, by the constant adjustments of the sheath and by turning the 'cipher to chaos direction' leading up to a 'lock state', then it shows how interpreting Indian-English requires a suspension of idiomatic thinking.

Indian-English is a favourite of small businessmen who use the language free of grammar or spelling rules to push their product. This notice, which was slipped in along with the newspapers, was printed by my neighbourhood beauty salon, The Beauty Care.

> With get a gold Jwellry
> Everry Hair and skin treatments with Impoted Machin
> Impoted makeup and nail art Centre
> New Year Special Packege
> For Bridal's
> Bridal and Prebridal and get Svgan Makeup free

The ad was issued by AR Marketing. I called them up to find out how they go about their business. And true to type and style, Anu Shukla, the man who owns the firm, was totally oblivious to the damage he had caused to spelling and grammar and proudly offered to do ads in any language. He informed me that he had five or six DTP operators who did his work. When I told him that one of his ads had too many mistakes, he said that the client must not have read the proofs properly but did not express any remorse, nor did he promise to do a fool-proof job in future. Utter confidence and bravado is the hallmark of all Indian-English users. It is this appropriation of the English language in some form that helps them ply their trade.

A year after AR Marketing issued this ad campaign, another beauty parlour in the neighbourhood started another campaign in English, slipping in their brochure with the newspaper. This one was issued by the Eden Woman Harbal Beauty Parloor. It might be an Eden for waxing, but for spelling and grammar it wasn't exactly paradise. It seemed that AR Marketing was at work here too.

The parlour was a blessing for bear-skinned women, I guess, because it was '7 Days Open' and specialized in removing hair from various nooks of the female body.

> Special cool Package
> A. Rs/310/-Full Arms wax Half Legs, Wax Face Bleach Fern Harbial Facial, Eyebrows, Forhead.
> B. Rs 500/-Full Arms Wax full legs, wax face+Neck Bleach Jolen Shahnaz or Silver Facial, Eyebrow Manicure Pedicure

After the first two cool package offers, Eden gets more confident and offers deforestation in other areas of the female anatomy but in doing so, converts the neck to neek and a Gold Facial appears as Go!d Facial, a mistake which now takes on a look of a typographical ploy.

> C. Rs 600 Full Arms legs wax under Arms Face +Neek, Jolen Bleach eyebrows, manicure pedicure Go!d Facial.

But even without the help of marketing agencies, the huge numbers of Indians who aspire to write in English have created their own vocabulary and thus enriched the language, much to the chagrin of purists and sticklers everywhere. Individual enterprise in this field can best be seen by going through matrimonial ads on a website, where the original ads are published without the interference of a cautious advertisement executive, a subeditor or a brand manager who is concerned about the language used in classifieds.

Here we can see the blend of Indian-English and internet and SMS jargon all coexisting in a good cause: the luring of a partner for life.

Websites like Shaadi.com and Bharatmatrimony.com are a haven for lonely hearts. The classifieds trying to win over women bring out the best in practitioners of Indian-English, for they are burdened with not just the task of putting together a sentence—an arduous task for most of them—but they have to be humourous and romantic and hip to boot. This multitask leaves many lonely men quite flabbergasted. But they carry on for their own sake and for the sake of the girls they hope to win over by their adherence to English.

> Hello to viewers, my name is shiva, I am single I don't have female. If any one want to marrie to me u can visite to my home. I am not a good education but I working all field in bangalroe…if u like me u welcome to my heart

Many writers, like Shiva, present themselves either as victim or achiever and, having done that, make demands from their prospective bride, like this young man who did not want his girl to drink and would allow her to wear jeans only in the house.

> I want a girl with no drinks if she wants she can wear jeans in house but while steping out of house she should give respect to our cast.

Or else she would be cast aside. Laying down the ground rules for the future seems to be a must with the ultramodern speaker of Indian-English. Feudal, moralistic, and with a paternal outlook to life in general, he has used the virtual world as a domain where he draws the line on female behaviour. To all that add the fact that many of them claim the ultimate trophy: they are handsome.

> Hye, I am a good loking boy, who has the capability to make any body to lough. I believe in god and according to me friends are the real messenger of God. The 3 things I am looking from a girl, they are 1. They must believe in God. 2. They have to like my profession and they should not get bored with me when I will try to make them lough.

We have no option but to lough a lot and hope that the guy takes in a gaud-loking girl. If the advertiser is not good-looking, he is happy-go-lucky, like this young man.

> I am a hapy-go-lucky kind of person. Enjoys every moments of life. I love to make friendship. Becauese friendship is a first step of love. I am looking for my dreamgirl who will love me more than i. Because I love myself a lot. If u think that is u then why to late come on…hold my hand forever!!!

But then what do guys who are neither handsome nor happy-go-lucky do? They obviously think that their knowledge of English is a positive factor that will let them rise above the 'phaltu peoples who try to be Bollywood hero and run away with sexy ladis'.

Some who are not handsome by their own estimate have various other options. One of them suggested that if the girl does not love him, she has the option of loving his mother. They, of course, resort to the old maxim that what matters is whether the heart is beautiful.

I want one girl who love me or my mother. She love me heartly or she have a frank skin colour 'normal' nor a black or not a whitey. I think the main think is heart if your heart is beautiful but I am not a handsome boy or not a good looking but my Mom says that I am a good boy. My father already expired. I am 'Aeklauta'. The choice is your.

With the last word, the unpretty man had a problem. Yes, the apostrophe, the bane of the English user. To say that the Indian-English user has no clue what purpose it serves is to be kind to him. Is it yours' or your's? But using the wisdom of a man who wants 'a frank skin normal' coloured lady, he decided to go in for the safe third option which is to drop the possessive 's' and the apostrophe altogether and stick with 'your'. At least he wouldn't lose a wife for the sake of a misplaced apostrophe.

Professionals too find the task of inserting a marriage ad quite daunting. One such professional from Chennai starting out trying to show that he had a soft heart that would melt at the sight of a pretty girl but achieved an effect that can be said to be quite contrary to his intentions since he is a 'businessman of granite' and hence we could surmise that he had a heart of stone.

I am an advocate and businessman of granite also. I wand working women in any privte or govt, but mostly like beauty and honesty natures.

If putting out ads in the hope of catching the attention of a pretty girl poses such problems for the aspiring Indian, then ads issued for wife-swapping also generate another set of problems. The word 'swap' and 'sex' cannot be used so easily. This particular report was reproduced in *India Today* of 15 June 1994. Two reporters of the magazine, pretending to be a couple, replied to such ads and then got into a swapping session. This ad (published in shady magazines) was reproduced in the article called 'Playing Mixed Doubles'. It is no surprise, then, that the advertiser presented himself as a decent person and not one looking to swap his wife.

> **About myself**: 39 years old, most decent in behaviour, married, employed in an electric company.
> **About liking**: I very much enjoy satisfying opposite sex, more than my personal satisfaction. I love to demonstrate/see people enjoying, can also join at request.

Though he was all set to be a swinger, the decent man found it fit to publicize under a separate subheading the major problems that faced him in his noble endeavour.

> **My Misfortune**: Non-cooperation from wife for swapping/orgy.

Once all the swappers got together, they sat around trying to start the action for the day, according to the report. They had different code words for sex. For the Malhotras it was 'enjoy', for the Gwalior couple it was 'programme' as in 'Heh, heh, so did you have a programme last night?' But let us draw a curtain over what happened next, as it wasn't 'propah', and didn't involve English either.

More than 200 years after the first of the Indian-English ads started appearing, this advertisement of 'Public Notice' from the government of Delhi's transport department was published in newspapers in New Delhi in early 2005. Awash in spelling mistakes and total governmental disdain for the basics of advertising or anything that is acceptable in language usage, the Delhi government's transport department held out this stunning specimen, a sort of glorious example of the growth, establishment, spread and clout of Indian-English.

1. Hounrable Supreme Court had ordered to Transport Department for registration of five thousand new CNG/LPG based Auto Rikshaws regarding the dispute No 13029 'M.C. Mehta versus Government of India' on dated 20-12-2005. department has reserved 2525 to general category, 750 to Schedule Caste 375 autorikshaws to Schedule Tribes and 1350 to other backward classses for registration. There are 407 positions are empty for other backward classes and 368 for Schedule Caste in the above reservation yet.

2. Application are inviting for the allotment of the above empty positions.

3. Applicant must have legal autorikshaw licence, autorikshaw Driver baz [this recent entrant to Ind-Eng vocabulary could have something to do with badge] and cast certificate of related reserved category. It will be compulsory to drive the autorikshaw by the applicant.

4. Applications can be obtained free from motor vehicle officer,…

5. The people who have applied previously they also should have apply secondly old application will not be entertained.

6. If the application will not have reached till date 25-2-2005 then department will have the right to convert the reserved category in to other category.

The bureaucrat has over the years been a champion of Indian-English. Though a Hindi advert would have sufficed, the babu often resorted to English, which I suspect is done in the hope that it would grab the attention of the anglicized higher-ups in the government. Wielding this formidable tool, the babu served as the crucial link between governance carried out in English and the masses, who knew only bits and pieces of the language of governance, or none at all. Intrepreting laws written in English to illiterate people was a duty that the babu took on with relish. Since the mountains of laws and regulations were all in the foreign tongue, the babu was the dada of all he surveyed. The babu preferred to use his version of English, the instance given above being a rip-roaring example. English language ads often became a handy ruse to prevent the common man from understanding rules or figuring out the nuances of new schemes for the poor and needy. This in turn helped the corrupt official and the middleman to fix jobs and tenders and give three-wheeler licences to his chosen men since the ad mentions as a matter of routine the right of the babu to reclaim those crucial posts by a change of category: 'the right to convert the reserved category in to other category'.

There was absolutely no need for this English advertisement targeted at the three-wheeler driver, not a single one of whom was likely to apply for the 'driver's baz' by accessing this ad in the *Hindustan Times*. But to advertise in English papers is always a way of letting the people concerned know that there is no hanky-panky in the grant of licences, while in fact the transport department has staff with the greasiest palms. The English advertisement is an acceptable façade for the manoeuvrings that go on behind the scenes.

Transport departments seem to be a repository of officials who have mastered Indian-English and use it at the slightest pretext. The principal secretary and commissioner of the transport department of the Uttaranchal government issued this unusual and intriguing advertisement in the *Hindustan Times* of 27 May 2005 advising drivers on the rules to be followed for driving on hill roads. Such advisories are not usual for transport departments, which specialize in issuing 'driver's baz'.

After mentioning norms like the wheel base and width of the vehicle the advisory goes on to give conditions for driver fitness.

10. Ensure that Driver is skilled and well experienced for hill roads. Drivers should be given only 8 hours steering duty at one stretch, after adequate rest, otherwise his fatigue may result into accident.

Then the principal secretary gets a bit steamy.

12. Driver should no consume any intoxication like alcohol etc. Drivers will be cheeked on breath analyzers of interceptors and if found intoxicated Steam action will be taken against such driver and vehicle owner.

To turn the steam on the driver would be a good idea, I guess, considering he is anyway hot under the collar most of the time. If the vehicle owner too is summoned for 'steam action', then a pressure-cooker atmosphere can be created by the transport department. A driver well-cooked and oiled is a good proposition for the ride up the hills, no doubt.

Not all government advertisements are as miserable. Such governmental intrusion into Indian-English has a long history like this 1939 Bombay Telephones ad in the *Bombay Chronicle,* trying to get people to use phones. 'Uncertainty can make life a nightmare' the heading went.

The gnawing anxiety of some crises in you home can seriously attack your day's business. Your thoughts stray involuntarily back to the sickbed and those around it.
KEEP IN TOUCH BY TELEPHONE

Straying limbs, not straying thoughts, were the concern of

railway officials of New Delhi station who were concerned about the safety of passengers who ventured to use the escalator. While the escalator is meant to help people climb stairs without the use of tired muscles, railway official seem to have torn asunder the sinews and limbs of the language in this long exhortation painted near the entrance to the escalator placed near platform 12 of the capital's main railway station. The ubiquitous sarkari babu, haughty and impatient in whatever he does, worked his magic here as well. I can imagine the office superintendent of some obscure railway department sitting down to the momentous task of framing the rules for use of escalators in railway stations and taking one month over it, with various underlings making alterations and suggestions and additions.

GUIDANCE FOR SAFE TRAVEL ON ESCALaTORS
1. While climbing escalators put right leg on moving stairs and hold handrail and put other leg immediately on moving stairs while climbing down put right leg on stationary plate and leave the handrail and put other leg on stationary plate
2. Coolies, porters person with heavy luggage/steel trunk/ are not permitted on escalators
3. Always face forward, do not run or jumps on or off the stairs
4. Do not lean against sides of escalators
5. Never sit or allow children to sit on the esecalators
6. Do not stand too close to the sides, sneakers and shoes can sink into the space between the steps and the side panel laces, boots, baggage and clothes can get caught in moving parts
7. Never walk up the escalator that is moving up or down
8. If you are wearing a saree, dhoti shawl or chunni make sure that there are no free flowing ends hold up the saree

or dhoti so that it cannot get entangled in the steps or side panels

9. Always hold children, old person and ill person by hand
10. If your shoelaces or any clothing gets caught, take it off immediately:-Abandon any be longing that gets caught Do not try to disentangle it by force

Here the numbering starts afresh, presumably because these are general suggestions.

1. During traveling, Do not throw cigarette butts tobacco and pan masala pouches, in to the gap
[Number missing]
3. If escalators are closed or luggage has fallen don get panicky
4. Journey on escalators without RA ticket/platfi ticket is prohibitted
5. Children below 8 years are not allowed to travel on moving escalators without guardian.

Governmental instructions to its citizens, mostly moral and punitive in nature, can be seen all over the country. Instructions start with one-liners written on walls ('Don spit') and go on, as we have seen, to long-winded instructions on 'how to use escalator'. There must be something basically wrong with governmental instructions because nothing seems to have worked and few rules are followed in India. Blame the language!

Over the last two centuries few, however, have tried Indian-English in print ads, though it is quite common in television ads. An in-house ad in the *Economic Times,* which ran through June and July 2006, put Indian-English to good use to sell sets of business communication CD-Roms.

We will continue to sapply profit to darling customers, holders of shares, staff-gentleman (also ladis) and the vendor type people.

Finally, the culprits: 'vendor-type people' who according to the common imagination are deemed to be the repositories of Indian-English. If only we could get hold of them, English could be purified with the yagna fires of Webster English.

The more things change, the more they remain the same. Today, district-level politicians too try to curry favour with the party president by issuing birthday greetings as English display ads on front pages of newspapers. Here is one in *The Hindu* of 18 May 2005. The general secretary of the Janata Dal (S), the ruling party in Karnataka, put out this ad in praise of his party president H. D. Deve Gowda, with the obvious hope that his efforts at reminding the national readership of his leader's great qualities (including how to 'risen from the dust'), would fetch him rewards in the future, at least in the form of a party ticket for the next elections.

> Shri H.D. Deve Gowda who never aspired the position of Prime Minister but did his best to serve the needs of the poor, was rewarded the post of Prime Minister in which Shri H.D. Devegowda excelled well in the available time. We pray the Almighty to empower this 'TRUE SON OF THE SOIL' who has 'ONCE AGAIN RISEN FROM THE DUST' with much more strength to compete his unfinished task.

To advertise in English is an Indian weakness. It embodies the need to he heard, seen and read by a higher class of people. The very nature of such advertising is aspirational and the use of English is very much a part of this national mindset. Not surprising therefore that all advertising from IAS tuition shops are in English, which follows the patterns detailed in this chapter. The language and the trend remain unchanged after all these years. The 14 October 2012 edition of *The Hindu* has this front page solus insertion aimed at IAS aspirants:

NEW DELHI IAS
Join and feel-the difference
    Be special different from crowd start serving nation from 2014
        Analyse, Precise, Pinpoint.

Through all this turmoil, Indian-English continues to grow and evolve.

4

THE LURE OF ENGLISH

How to get English to roll off your tongue! You know
English. You write good English…But do you speak
it fluently? Easily & continuously without unwanted
h-e-s-i-t-a-t-i-o-n-s?
—Advertisement for English conversation
coaching

The spread of English—in any form—was a juggernaut that
couldn't be stopped since Indians craved English as a 'higher
language'. After independence, its importance and relevance did
not diminish but increased. This effort ran parallel and counter
to the government's efforts to give an impetus to the use of
Hindi all over the country. For, the government was justifiably
worried about the power wielded by English as the official and
written language. Jawaharlal Nehru, of course, was instrumental
in preventing a total ban on English by arguing that a language
cannot be forced on the people. He rightly suspected that
the south would not accept Hindi as the official language. As

expected, when the pro-Hindi stance of the Central government boomeranged and a violent anti-Hindi agitation started in the south, English sneaked in as a ready-made alternative. If English hadn't caught on, Indian-English too would have withered away, without periodical drip feeding from its fount of inspiration. Back in the nineteenth century, the promotion of the language was done under British pressure. The colonials had felt an urgent need to compile records in English, something they did with fanatic verve, as we know. These records had to be in English; once that was achieved there was little option for local governments but to follow suit.

Much thought and ink went into forcing the propagation of the language. A letter to the Viceroy from London dated 12 May 1880 *(Linguistic and Oriental Essays)* laid down specific benchmarks, stressed the importance of vernacular languages, and suggested ways of slowly squeezing in English:

> I trust that this important subject will be attended to: it is important both to the Administrative and Educational Department. It is suggestive of great existing injustice if the Courts of Justice are not supplied with officials capable of speaking the vernaculars of the people; the forced use of Hindi or other dominant vernacular is to be deprecated. The Central provinces contain more than a million Gond-speaking people, yet not one Gond-School exists. There may be many cases in the Courts of Justice where language is used totally unintelligibly to the Judicial or Executive Officer, and yet there are no paid interpreters. The greatest care should be taken in enforcing the use of the same terminology, the absolute exclusion of Vernacular terms, as well as technical and official phraseology and the maintenance of the same orthography for proper names through the Empire.
>
> There is no reason why English terms should not be

adopted to describe the subdivision of jurisdiction, the Courts of Justices, the rank of officials and the operations of Commerce, Manufacture and Agriculture.

Very stringent rules should be laid down as to what vernacular word as Rupee etc may be admitted. Weights, measurements, distance must be expressed in English terms if they are to be of any statistical value...

Stringent rules were indeed laid out, spellings of Indian towns and words categorized and various efforts made to rein in Indian pronunciation. In all this we can see the British fascination for detail, something totally absent among Indians. Volume 23 of the *Imperial Gazetteer* published in 1908 had a detailed observation about Indian consonants and how these have been tackled. In all this, one sees an attempt to put together a framework to tackle quotidian improbabilities and concerns.

Most Indian languages have different forms for a number of consonants such as d, t, r, and e marked in scientific work by the use of dots or italics. As the European ear distinguishes these with difficulty, in ordinary pronunciation it has been considered undesirable to embarrass the reader with them and only two notes are required...In the first place the Arabic K, a strong guttural has been represented by 'k' instead of 'q' which is often used. Secondly it should be remarked that aspirated consonants are common and in particular 'dh' and 'th' (except in Burma) never have the sound of 'th' in 'this' but should be pronounced as in 'woodhouse' and 'boat hook'.

The names of some places—Calcutta, Bombay, Lucknow, Cawnpore—have obtained popular fixity of spelling while special forms have been officially prescribed for others. Names of persons are often spelt and pronounced differently in different parts of India but the variations have been made as few as possible by assimilating forms and almost especially

where a particular spelling has been generally adopted in
English books...

While many such instructions were issued and carried out
to perfection over the years, it is interesting to see how various
lobbies worked in India to spread the use of English. Such
lobbying gave to the language a legitimacy even in independent
India, when everything connected with the Raj was sought to be
done away with—statues, road names and all such removables.
The pro-English debate was more passionate in Madras state
(later Tamil Nadu), where this demand neatly dovetailed into
the anti-Hindi agitation. Better to use English than Hindi was
the war cry of the Tamilians, and this had reverberations in
other southern states as well. The Hindi versus English debate
was actually a north versus south debate. So English, in a way,
had the support of nearly half the country. Clinging to the coat-
tails of English, Indian-English learned to find its way. Anyway,
there was this under-class of people who used the Indianized
form of English—confidently, lavishly and elaborately, in
hoardings, ads, and letters—and had already made Indian-
English into an accepted form, a stepping stone to acceptance
and legitimacy.

Well-known Gandhian C. F. Andrews in his biography of
educationist and reformer *Zaka Ullah Khan of Delhi* (W. Heffer
and Sons Ltd, Cambridge) also points to the inner conflict
among social reformers about the use of English:

> After leaving the Old Delhi college and passing through
> many vicissitudes, Munshi Zaka Ullah, entered the
> education department of the Government of India. It was
> in this connection that he began seriously to study English,
> employing the help of a teacher. By sheer hard work, though

beginning his study of English after middle ages had passed by, he acquired in time the ability to read difficult English books. But he was never able to speak the language fluently and very rarely attempted to do so even for a short time. His mastery of English literature, however was extensive; and he was at all times an omnivorous reader of English books and periodicals.

Zaka Ullah personified the Janus-faced attitude educated Indians had towards English. Many preferred English as a language of writing and reading, not for speaking a few lilting words or raising a toast at social dos. Others tried to show that they knew the language by using a few sentences when they were in elite company. English lurked everywhere, but there was a general coyness about embracing it wholeheartedly, though with the wisdom of hindsight we can now say that this inner dilemma of Indians was resolved quite satisfactorily: English grew by leaps and bounds, but so did the popularity of Hindi, and out of this encounter, and despite all the guilt and the anti-national label that English was stamped with, the illegitimate child Indian-English fattened.

While being an 'omnivorous reader' of English books, Zaka Ullah cautioned the people against the…

… constant use of English even from our childhood so that we begin to express our thoughts in it, instead of in our mother tongue, will go far to denationalize us. If we wish to remain as Eastern people we must not neglect the language which we learnt at our mothers' knee. We must not become foreigners to our own population and practically to all our women folk. Our mother tongue contains for us all our hallowed memories and traditions; it is our first articulate speech which we employ while talking to our mothers when we are young. To forget it or to despise it is to lose one of the strongest factors in the building up of national character.

Zaka Ullah foresaw a grave danger: Indians despising their own mother tongue. He was right: children throughout urban India are reprimanded by their ambitious, go-getting mothers for speaking in their mother tongue and not in correct English. The intrusion of Hindi into this new Indian urban English is a sort of comeuppance.

So the yearning for English often and naturally conflicted with the need to build national character. Out of this conflict was born the via media, Indian-English, which too grew alongside, unhindered and unpatronized but now threatening to take over cinema and advertising. After the Pepsi Indian-English catchline '*Yeh dil maange* more' (this heart craves for more) became a hit, English words have become a must in Hindi advertising—like the corny ICICI adline: 'No *chinta, sirf money*'.

The intrusion of, or acceptance of, Hindi or Hinglish is now nationalized mainly due to English supplements of national newspapers working on the assumption that the iPod generation prefers to 'cut the crap' and go straight to the heart of the matter in local lingo.

'Attention, wannabe new age *netas;* India's first P-school (P *bole toh,* politics) is ready to train you in value-based governance. Delhi Times on a neo school of thought…' runs such a wonky strapline.

This reverse swing of Hindi into English is a new millennium phenomenon, driven by the success of Hindi catchlines in advertising and the titles of Bollywood movies which in any case easily pass on to everyday speech.

But the attempt to have Indian titles or catchlines has landed Indian companies in deep shit, literally. An apple juice company renamed their product 'Appy', which in Malayalam and Tamil slang means excreta. Appy still sells in the south, as I realized, but advertising created a problem: 'Thirsty? Sip Appy, so slurpy'. Quite turdish, a Madrassi would say. If by any chance Appy reaches record sales, the catchline which would capture the attention of all those in the south would run like this: 'The Biggest Appy: thank you for sipping it all the way'.

But the effort to establish English in post-independence India was not easy. Debates, which still continue, started soon after independence, some of which reflected Jawaharlal Nehru's concern about forcing people to use Hindi.

To give an illustration of the efforts made to emphasize the role of English in independent India, I give below excerpts from a seminar on 'The Place of English in an Educational System' held on 4-5 November 1967 in the Centenary Auditorium of the University of Madras.

The object of the seminar was to 'promote good and adequate knowledge of the English language at all levels of education'. Though the seminar was meant to focus on education, what happened was a call to accept English as the working language everywhere in India. All speakers gave poor marks to Indian languages when comparing them to English. In fact, most speakers wrote off Indian languages as unfit to serve the calling of a techno-savvy future.

Sir A. Ramaswami Mudaliar said in his welcome address:

> We have said that in the school and in the college there is a place for English. It is through that language that we can get at the senior stages, at higher reaches of learning, all that vast treasure of wisdom and knowledge which is growing so rapidly from day to day and so enriching our thought, our ideas, our knowledge—experimental and otherwise, even

our philosophies which are ancient can be enriched by the
philosophic knowledge of the English-speaking world…

For travel, for international work, for industry, for all of
them English is necessary…

I would suggest that in the school stage also English should
be made a compulsory subject…

Note the juxtaposition of English as the language of modern
times, the language of technology, with Indian languages which
are 'ancient', quite unlike English, 'which is growing so rapidly
from day to day…' Mudaliar went on to make a high-adrenalin
pitch for English, apart from presenting himself as a victim of
ridicule by those who did not speak the language.

Ladies and gentlemen, we who know the English language
are being accused of all sorts of things. I have borne many of
them…we are told that we are snobs speaking in the English
language, frightening ordinary people…

Then he went on to present English once again as the language
of modern times and the medium of technology. 'Nearly 150
years ago, it was Raja Rammohan Roy who pleaded for English
schools to be run with what little money the East India Company
had left for them so that their children might benefit thereby.
After 150 years what is the stage of English today? In 1900, there
were only 2,50,000 words in the English language. Now there
are 6,63,000', he announced triumphantly.

Another speaker, K. Subba Rao, adopted a more hectoring
tone. Like the speaker before him, he valiantly defended the
continued use of English: 'What would be the result of replacing
English by the fifteen languages in the High Court and the
Supreme Court? The Indian legal field will become a veritable
babel of voices. Laws will be in fifteen languages and the Central

laws, arguments and judgements of the Supreme Court will be in Hindi.'

Frank Antony, well-known legal luminary and Anglo-Indian member of Parliament for a long time, mocked at the efforts of the government to marginalize English. 'Mr Morarji Desai wants to create a vacuum in the educational system by ousting English and wishes that vacuum to be filled by Hindi...' Antony went on to use logic which would have sounded novel at that time. 'It is no good arguing that English is a foreign language. In fact, English is even foreign to the British. It was a Saxon language for the ancestors of Britain. English is foreign only in a limited sense, in the sense that relatively it is foreign to India.'

The foreignness of the language having been rubbished, other speakers then continued to glorify English: 'Without English how would it be possible for our Ramaswami Mudaliar and Lakshmanswami Mudaliar to attend international conferences...' one of them stated. This was logic that could be heard over and over again as the debate raged in India over the years.

Then Sir M. A. Muthiah Chettiar went on to narrate how at a meeting in Trichy at the eighty-ninth birthday celebrations of Ramaswami Naicker, the patron of the Dravida movement, the people rooted for English. 'I had the privilege of inaugurating and Anna presided. Hundreds and thousands of people—there were about two lakh people in the procession who could not reach the meeting for want of space... Students were exhorted to read English. Everbody applauded the exhortation...'

In such gatherings, students too got a chance to stake their claim to inherit the English legacy. Kumari Durga Kidao was among the speakers at this pro-English seminar—and if at all there were any doubts that youngsters were in two minds about using English, Kidao's forceful presentation would have laid them to rest. She fully endorsed the 'English line' of the earlier speakers, starting out with the theory that English was the mother of all languages.

1. It is one of the most flexible of languages. Having imbibed the influence of various literatures it is now the essence of Greek, Latin, Spanish, German and several others. It is ever changing. Its flexibility has rendered it ideal for universal usage…

6. Of course our mother tongues are beautiful. But they are evolved in a different context and for a different purpose. They are ideal for expressing subtle nuances of human feelings and emotion. But they cannot be used for all purposes.

7. English on the other hand is unrivalled for its presentation of facts in the simple beauty of its expression and for its appeal to the widest range of human interests.

The post-independence debate on the use of English constantly compared the regional languages to English and found it wanting. The pro-English camp presented English as a language of universal communication and conferred on the language powers it did not possess. To argue, like Durga, that regional languages cannot be used for higher purposes was the done thing.

The same debate raged in elite literary salons in the early days of British rule. The debate was often tinged with guilt, for how could an Indian support the language of the colonists? How would backing English impact the national movement?

'The desire to use language as a sign of national identity is a very natural one, and in consequence language has played a prominent part in national movements. Men have often felt the need to cultivate a given language to show that they are distinct from another race whose hegemony they resent', wrote

Randolph Quirk in *The Use of English,* which is a prescribed text in many Indian universities.

In India there was resentment among some people against English, but this was softened by the adulation others heaped on the language. English was an ally in the fight against Hindi domination which raged in Chennai and Assam. 'English— formerly much identified with foreign rule—is paradoxically the only language which tends to encourage unity and discourage separatist movements', Quirk rightly wrote. There are various views on this, of course, but the national debate on the subject has been healthy and has finally led to the dual stream English- Hindi usage.

This debate or this conflict started and raged mostly in Bengal, where British English first put down firm roots, thanks to Bengali proponents of English and the region's bilingual literary giants. One of the architects of this mid-nineteenth century English literary efflorescence was poet Michael Madhusudan Dutt (1824-73) who wrote this eulogy for English:

> I acknowledge to you, I need not blush to do so—that I love
> the language of the Anglo-Saxon. Yes—I love the language—
> the glorious language of the Anglo-Saxon. My imagination
> visions forth before me the language of the Anglo-Saxon in all
> its radiant beauty; and I feel silenced and abashed.

The English-Bengali encounter is fascinating to follow, especially considering the fall-out—timeless works in both languages. Even though Bengali literature was having its big moments, many of its architects were not willing to give the language its due at that stage. In 1872, Bankimchandra Chattopadhyay gave another gilt-edged certificate to English in the first issue of the Bengali magazine *Bangadarshan:* 'There is one outstanding barrier to the writing of Bengali by educated Bengalis. Educated people do not read Bengali and what educated people will not read educated people do not wish to write.' Bankimchandra's first novel, *Rajmohan's Wife,* was written in English, though he went on to pen some of the most well-known fiction in Bengali.

A letter which was published in the *Times of India* of 19 February 1883 showed that the urge to popularize English permeated the country and was not just limited to islands of literary affluence like Bengal. The letter titled 'A Society for Speaking English' appealed for the facilitation of an English society:

> Many young natives, and particularly Parsees, now-a-days show a great desire to acquire the habit of correctly, elegantly and fluently speaking English and no doubt they should, since to be able to speak well is an ornamental and useful art. But with all their anxiety they do not seem actually to have the heart to realize their desire. Speaking well is one of the fine arts and it can be pursued as a diversion from studies and other occupations. But there is also another difficulty in attaining it and that is the utter want to means—there are no clubs or societies for practicing and cultivating it. The need has long been felt and I think the professors of Dr Wilson's College who are known to be arduously working in the cause of the education of the young men of the city must be looked to for assistance in this matter. If these gentlemen should take up the matter, I think the professors of the Elphinstone College might also kindly come forward and join them in their praiseworthy endeavours. What they may at the outset do would be to invite members (who should not be school-boys) to a society for the culture and improvement of oral English and if the invitation is largely responded to, they will know how to proceed further.
>
> 19th February 1883   PRUDENS FUTURI

The English versus local language debate still continues, though in the search for global positioning Indians no longer want to be seen as a Hindi-speaking nation, like the Japanese are a Japanese-speaking nation. English, in fact, is now considered a national asset, even though there still remains a department for the spread of Hindi: it tries to translate official documents into Hindi and issues occasional exhortations to motivate babus to use Hindi.

The use of English does not make Indians guilty any longer, and the facile way in which Indians take to English has made it the magnet of outsourced jobs. It will take China and other Asian giants a long time to catch up with or match either the numbers or the standard of English in India. In recent times, the Phillipines has emerged as a centre for outsourced call centres and other such Business Process Outsourcing centres. Filipino companies have managed to undercut Indian companies. But then, India has a larger and better pool of people capable of working in English and so there is always the possibility of high-skill jobs coming to India.

English assumes various forms in different regions, so there cannot be any real faulting of usage or regional interpretation. There is nothing really that can be called standard English, unless it is the English used by the educated Brit as opposed to that used by Americans. The problem now is that more non-Brits than citizens of Britain speak English.

Indian-English, for all our contempt, is set to get wide acceptance in India. In hoardings, advertisements and movies, Indian-English is already, without doubt, the accepted form. With its own bizarre grammar, spelling and vocabulary, Indian-English is well set to rule the country, having defeated the Queen's English in a centuries-long battle. Of course, this triumph is not unique to Indian-English alone, and all localized variations of

English, be it Asian or Latin American, have seen this parallel growth—but nowhere is the local English patois as significant and influential as in India. The difference is in the number of people who understand and use the form, and for whom Indian-English is a stepping stone to bigger things.

Off and on, efforts are made and clarion calls issued by educationists to take to correct English. But as globalization spreads and outsourced jobs become the vogue, India is confident it is very much in the picture, despite its adoption of Indian-English. There is a critical mass of 'correct' English-speaking people. What worries the Singapore prime minister is not what should concern the Indian prime minister. 'Speak in full sentences with proper sentences and cutting out all the *lars* and *lors* at the end of each sentence,' Singapore Prime Minister Lee Hsien Loong exhorted his people on 12 May 2005. 'It is important for all of us to speak good English, because English has become the lingua franca of international commerce,' he said. 'English is our bridge to the world,' he said, clearly worried at the spread of Singlish with its varied Chinese and Tamil influences—and queasy tags at the end of sentences which he winced at.

A *Newsweek* report in its March 2005 issue predicted, quoting a British Council report, that 'Within a decade, 2 billion people will be studying English and about half the world—some 3 billion people—will speak it.' As debated here, the new English speakers will continue to shape the language, even though we would love to smirk at them. The new English speakers aren't just passively absorbing the language—they're shaping it. New Englishes are mushrooming the globe over, ranging from 'Englog', the Tagalog-infused English spoken in the Philippines, to 'Japlish', the cryptic English poetry beloved of Japanese copywriters ('Your health and loveliness our best wish', read a candy wrapper. 'Give us a chance to realize it'), to 'Hinglish', the mix of Hindi and English that now crops up everywhere from fast-food ads to South Asian college campuses.

In an article titled 'Lingua Franker' (the *Times of India*, 21 May 2005), well-known humour-writer and journalist Jug Suraiya commented on the call of the Singapore prime minister for correct English, wondering whether there is something called correct usage. 'Libertarians, however, would argue that language, any language, is not about correctness but about communication. And often you can communicate more effectively by bending or breaking rules of grammar and vocabulary.' Jug mentioned the case of the campaign: 'Don't rubbish Hong Kong'—a big success. 'It was bad English but good communication', he wrote.

> Lee Hsien Loong was only partly right when he said that English was the language of international commerce. Language is commerce. It is a free trade agreement of ideas and feelings. The fewer official restrictions on the trade, the greater the benefits for all. So who decides what is English as it ought to be spoken or as she should be spoke?

English, no doubt, has a great market in India, where 30 million people, according to Suraiya's figures, speak English. What kind of English they speak is a different matter.

The only official statistics available about the English-speaking habits of Indians can be seen in the Indian Retirement Earnings and Savings Survey (IRES) conducted by the department of finance in 2004-2005. This survey of earners only showed that 35 per cent of them claimed to know how to read English and 16.5 per cent knew how to speak English.

In the 20-30 years age group which forms a quarter of India's earners, 10 per cent can read English, while Hindi readers are at 14 percent. Only 16.5 per cent can speak English, but many more—35 per cent—can read. In the case of Hindi, 31 per cent can speak and 51.5 per cent can read as well.

Though it is not politically correct for politicians to ask Indians to take to proper English and 'speak in full sentences', many officials and educationists have tried their luck. In Patna University, not best known for its English users or writers, the pro-vice chancellor Dr S. Ehteshmuddin refused the application of a student who could not spell 'Controller of Examinations'. The student had a Master's degree in surgery, the *Hindustan Times* of 15 May 2005 reported. The university proctor, Dr Kritesh Prasad, annoyed by a misspelt application, asked an English honours student to spell 'Shakespeare', 'principal' and 'sincerely'. What he got was 'Sexpeer', 'principle' and 'seriously'.

Such efforts reflect the frustration of guardians of the Queen's English, but nothing seems to hinder the growth of Indian-English. Debates rage, seminars are held, languages are linked to the freedom movement and national culture, departments for the propagation of Hindi are set up, flags of nationalism are raised, authors talk of guilt and conflict of interests, national languages are pitted against each other—but, as if cloistered from all that is going on, the Indian version of English grows. No one speaks on its behalf, no grammarians accept its parentage, no student openly backs Indian-English usage like Durga Kidao did for English in Chennai in 1965, though many students work hard to master it or at least yearn to use it. Streetside painters dab it on walls and hoardings, roadside shopkeepers proudly display Indian-English on their boards, writers (yeah, this writer included) launch into theories and paeans and monographs on Indian-English, quacks and astrologers (as we have seen) find it a handy communication tool, in Bollywood cameos Indian-English is quite a hit. Borrowing bits and pieces of its genetic code from its parent, reworking spellings, literally translating phrases and metaphors, often creating words, relentlessly frustrating efforts to sort it out, these mostly unseen, unsung patrons of Indian-English continued to hold aloft its flag. Like Madhusudhan Dutt, they are in the race to embrace the Anglo-Saxon language, but unlike him can be said to have consistently fallen behind. To turn around Bankimchandra's clincher, Indian-English was what the uneducated people wrote for the benefit of the educated. Those well-educated and conversant in Indian regional languages are not considered educated enough till they can roll their 'r's well and spin grandiose phrases. The huge masses of such well-read and educated people are not given their due place at the high table until they get their English right. This remains the great Indian paradox. Even as I was writing this chapter, I saw during an evening ride through Delhi a banner strung out across a flyover near the capital's ITO intersection. The bridge overlooks one of the busiest traffic intersections in the world. The banner was an anti-English poster hastily written in Hindi and after exhorting people to speak only in Hindi said that English speakers were *'deshdrohis'* (anti-national, or unpatriotic). Paradoxically and not surprisingly the name of the organization which was campaigning was Public Union. The anti-English founder of the group, which did not seem to have any other immediate intention other than issuing threats to English speakers, does not seem to have applied his mind to thinking up a name for his group, and the irony of using an English name must not have struck home. That is because both 'public' and 'union' are accepted words in Hindi as well, and few realize that they are English.

Hindi, like English, is a free borrower of words—and that could be the reason for the huge popularity of both languages. 'Police public *ko bahut tang karta hai'*, (the police harasses the public) 'Public *ko kya mila*' (what did the people get?), etc. 'Public' is an all-encompassing word as soon as it is used in Hindi and can be used to refer to the underprivileged masses, victimized people, mute spectators, vote banks. The word public has also the aura of victimhood about it, making it an immensely useful word to be dragged out and flaunted during speeches. Many politicians fight to represent the 'public' and campaigners often talk about the needs of the 'public'.

Newspapers are filled every day with hastily written advertisements from the police departments of various states and the CBI 'informing the general public' about a crook whose grainy mugshot is published alongside as proof not only of Indian studio photography's rise but also as proof of the efficiency of the department concerned.

Over the years the average Indian, the 'public' and 'the general public', so to say, has tried his or her best to master the spoken and written form of English and a fair amount of success has been achieved. Students are constantly reminded about the need to speak English to get anywhere in life, corporates are advised to have English-speaking courses to achieve success in business deals, and for girls, of course, it is important to be heard to be English-speakers for a better chance of betrothal. Another frequent invocation of the word 'general public' is seen in classified ads, where legal disputes are sought to be settled or when lawyers and solicitors are daggers drawn about property or the use of a trademark. This lawyer's ad tucked amid the clutter of a Hindi daily was at pains to inform the 'general public' that some members of a family have been cut off from the family legacy. Such ads are frequent, and as the history of classified ads shows [see earlier chapter], people tend to follow the pattern set by earlier advertisers. Also, such inheritance ads adopt almost the same phraseology.

PUBLIC NOTICE
Known to all general public that my clientess Smt Beena
Devi, wife of Late Parmod Kumar Sharma, R/O 1/424, Nand
Nagri, Delhi disowned her relations from her son namely
Arvind Kumar Bhalu son of Late Sh. Parmod Kumar Sharma
R/O as above in all manners and has debarred him from her
movable and immovable property. If any body deals him in
future for his misdeeds, acts etc, He shall be liable and my
client shall not be liable for the same.

It might be a bit too early to say that the ongoing tussle between
Bharat and English has been decided in favour of the latter.
Angry letters are still written to newspapers in English, attacking
the effort to run down Hindi. On 25 June 2005, an email from
Shivam Lakhampal appeared in the *Times of India* under the
heading 'Colonial legacy' propounding the well-known theory
about the slave mentality and cloying sentimentality when it
came to English.

This is with reference to Hashim Kidwai's letter 'Anti-English';
Kidwai calls Mulayam Singh's anti-English stance narrow-
minded. It shows our colonial mindset. We Indians seem to
have an inferiority complex. As a result, Sanskrit lies extinct
today and Hindi is slowly fading out. Japan, France, Germany
and Russia which take great pride in their languages, are
amongst the most developed countries in the world. Clearly,
English is not the key to development.

The irony is that Lakhampal himself writes in English,
suggesting that it is the language of convenience for him too.
His whole-hearted support for Indian languages (Sanskrit but
not Urdu) and his emailing of the letter suggests that he is
most probably settled abroad, and as such has opted to be in

an English-language environment—and would most probably have flaunted his knowledge of English to get a job. The longing to help Indian languages and the need to specialize in English to earn a living at the same time has been a major aspect of this great Indian linguistic paradox.

That is why in every town there are English conversation coaching institutes which offer everything from 'fluency in English' and 'confidence in career' to 'big prospects for career advancement'. An entire education industry has sprung up around the Indian need to know English. Many such courses and institutes are corporatized and are by all indications making a good business of it. One such company called Fluentzy offers itself as the 'world's 1st & most time-honoured system of fluency building'. The Fluentzy teaching company took out a full-page advertisement feature in *The Hindu* in April 2005 (the month when students are deciding what course of study to undertake). *Newsweek* estimates that the English teaching industry in India alone is at an annual $100 million, or about ₹450 crore.

The Fluentzy advertisement feature offers everything that an aspirational India would be looking for. 'How to get English to roll off your tongue!' 'You know English. You write good English…. But do you speak it fluently? Easily & continuously without unwanted h-e-s-i-t-a-t-i-o-n-s?'

One among the twenty books that the course offers is called *Fluency Building and Mouth Gymnastics*. To present English as a complicated language which requires the tongue and the mouth to indulge in some pirouetting and high vaults is part of the elaborate paraphernalia which surrounds the teaching and learning of English in India. The course promises various strategies for teaching English and makes out that it has some magic formula which will overcome imponderable hurdles to learning the language.

INEXHAUSTIBLE FLUENCY SOURCE
Mind you. True fluency is not the speed of delivery of speech.
No it isn't. It's something wholly different. Something whose
mark is really effortlessness. Fluent English is the ready flow
of speech units. A steady stream of word clusters flowing out
easily, from something called the fluency nucleus.

An advert on the same page by the Adult Faculties Council
too offers Fluency Prospectus, hopefully the same thing as the
hyped-up 'Fluency course'. The aim of the Adult Faculties
Council based in Kochi is 'unifying the world—thro fluent
English'. Some similarity here with the intentions of the
Singapore prime minister.

In all the small and big towns which I visited to research this
book, I could see that spoken English was big business. With
much use of jargon and obfuscation, students were promised a
transformation into English-speaking students, from just 'BA
MA pass'. Since the standard of English in small-town colleges
are not up to the mark, external help is offered, mostly given by
self-proclaimed professors of and experts in English.

In Thaliparambha, Kerala, one such English-speaking academy
advertised its services as 'The Doorway to English' and just to
make sure that its English-aspirant audience understood what it
meant, gave the Malayalam translation alongside. Know-How
publications in the village of Thalimparamba had published *A
Complete and Comprehensive Guide to English Grammar and
Spoken English*.

When I spoke to him, Joseph Mathew, who thought up this
academy, seemed to be a man in a hurry. In his voice there was
the urgency of a man who realizes that his business model may,
after all, work. Mathew said that he was busy preparing for a trip
to the Gulf where he hopes to sell some of his spoken English

guides and start his crash courses there and 'teach communication skills to executives there'. He wasn't obviously going there to teach the Arabs but the large population of Malayalees who have started treating the Persian Gulf countries as their El Dorado, a glittering desert outpost of infinite possibilities. Mathew was one among those who, having made a mark in Kerala, immediately took the flight out to the Gulf to present his credentials to the expat Malayalee population. He was thus following the path of politicians, priests and artists who are now mostly found touring the Gulf to gain acceptance and, if possible, financial assistance from the Kerala expats.

Mathew dodged a question about whether he was a professor of English, but said that in two years he had trained many nurses to speak English, batches of twenty students at a time. He charges ₹5,000 for three months just for spoken English.

English teaching factories spread over the towns, villages and cities of India could add a substantial amount to the GDP if they are classified under the manufacturing sector. Considering that many degree shops and fake universities sell degrees, it is not too distant a possibility.

In Noida city, fast emerging as a glitzy mall megalopolis bordering Delhi, I walked into an English teaching institution with the almost generic name that such shops use: British School of Education. A pretty young thing was at the front office, which seemed otherwise unoccupied. The shop, of course, did not have any brochures, which makes it easier for rates to be 'adjusted'. Among the English-speaking courses that it offered were British Smart, which would take forty-five days, and British Confident, which would take seventy-five. The list of all such courses and possibilities written on a piece of paper was offered to me. The receptionist did not have the name of any of the teachers, nor could she say whether they had proper qualifications.

There was another list of courses which would teach only conversation. The course included Tongue Twisters, Group Discussions, Debates and Extempore. Candidates were also mentally wrestled into taking a course which would cost more than ₹3,000 for two months. The Tongue Twister course sounds similar to the Mouth Gymnastics of the Fluentzy course. To present English as a language that calls for a lot of trapeze acts is part of the mystifying technique the English teaching shops use everywhere.

Such institutes situated mostly in the commercial hub of Indian cities are looking at capitalizing on the English craze. English is, of course, linked to upward mobility, and those at the lower rungs see an English certificate from the British School of Education as a step up the ladder. A young man who had entered the English shop soon after I did said he wanted to study computers, since it would help him improve his career prospects. He had come because the banner said English is essential for computer courses. He was a lawyer's clerk.

Clerk or MBA, many Indians feel the need to be more vocal in English. Who are these educated people who line up to learn English, and why?

Arun Ganapathy, one of India's leading language training consultants, lays out several reasons. The predominant one is that the home environment keeps out English. '"At home they don't even let us watch television programmes in English," most of the students tell me when I suggest that watching English programmes may help them,' Ganapathy says.

So while a degree is a must in most of these houses, English is seen as secondary goal, so to say, until they get a degree and then ask themselves, 'What now?'

Ganapathy is also member of the British Council's travelling faculty for educating English teachers across India with the help of state governments. Frequent courses for English teachers are held in Patna, for instance, where English teachers who have only rudimentary knowledge of the language are brought together to a hotel or conference centre and efforts are made to bring them to the next level. The standard of English teaching in small towns is appalling according to Ganapathy.

Most Indian graduates have had no exposure to English conversation beyond rote learning in school, as a result of which they have difficulty at the university level—the ages below fifteen or seventeen years are considered best to acquire language skills. Graduates would have studied college courses in English, but they would not have acquired fluency in the langauge. Even when it comes to the workplace, communication is in Hindi or the local language even if the job requires an English-speaking employee. So with an English environment missing everywhere, most highly qualified Indians find themselves out of place. They make do with whatever form of Indian-English they can muster while writing English.

Ganapathy, who sits in at presentations in multinational companies based in New Delhi and Mumbai, observes that only one or two engineers do the talking while the other five or six, who are highly qualified as well, just sit and listen, especially if there are foreigners in the meeting or in video conference. An environment dominated by English, quite common in most companies now, silences a majority of Indians. This could be the case in any country; but in few other places is the urge to get into the English-speaking bracket as urgent and demanding as in India. When opportunity knocks, English is the key.

'The reading and writing is well structured in school and colleges. The professor does not talk in English most of the time since he himself has never been taught to communicate in English,' says Ganapathy.

The irony is that while being skilled in English conversation is not necessary to get technical jobs, it boosts confidence levels and helps in moving up the hierarchy. Since passive knowledge of English is high among non-speakers, a two- or three-month course in English, which professionals like Ganapathy offer, is often enough to boost confidence levels and help them use the language at work, at the very least.

5

MISSIVES AND OTHER PUBLIC NUISANCES

The book 'Vade-Mecum' is my needy choice. For a
long spell it has been on a wild goose-chase. Could you
please mind me and mend the torn hope?
          —Letter from reader to a weekly paper

When it comes to putting pen to paper, Indians prefer
English. As the nation stumbled from one crisis to
another, or achieved the occasional triumph, people around
the country found writing letters to the editor in English the
best way of catching the attention of the ruling elite—the same
reasoning which led quacks and other traders to turn to English
advertising.

Another subject created much excitement among readers,
and that was cricket. Some of the early letters that appeared
in Indian journals were about the game. With the benefit of
hindsight, we can now say that these early letters foretold the

way the sport would capture the imagination of Indians. The letter with which I start this chapter is not necessarily a classic example of Indian-English but contains many phrases that an Indian would use. Many such letters in the early days of Indian journalism laid the foundation for a wealth of literature that cricket was to produce. They also give us an idea of how the game captured the imagination of Indians at a time when it was just taking root in England. Such letters also opened up new possibilities to newspaper readers. Interacting with the elite through the English newspaper was soon to become a habit with the emerging English readership.

The cricket enthusiast who preferred to call himself 'Wicket Keeper' could possibly have been a Bengali gentleman. A majority of those who wrote to editors preferred pen-names, for reasons I can only guess at. The hiding of identity helped Indian writers when it came to competing for space with Englishmen, who too wrote letters and would naturally have been given preference. The subterfuge also saved them the blushes if someone pointed out wrong usages and helped them escape the wrath of authorities. The first sentence of this letter from 'The Wicket Keeper' in *The Englishman and Military Chronicle* of January 1857 uses 'perhaps as'—not a beginning that an Englishman would have preferred. The letter had no blatant instances of Indian usages but the metaphor and imagery is interesting enough. 'The Wicket Keeper' may rightly claim to also have been one of India's first cricket correspondents.

Sir,

Perhaps as this is the first instance in which young Bengal has shown any interest in the manly game of Cricket, you will kindly give space in your columns for the following short account of a Match that we played on the Chinsurah ground between the students of the Hoogly and Kishnaghur College.

The Hoogly clubs having sent a challenge to the Kishnaghur lads about five weeks ago, it was at once accepted and both sides have been every evening in tolerably active practice. The Kishnaghur eleven with many of their fellow students arrived at Chinsurah on Christmas Day and the next morning, after the annual prizes had been distributed, there was a general move towards the cricket ground. The handsome dresses of the Hoogly eleven was much admired and it served to set off their figures to much advantage. They exhibited more bone and sinew that their opponents who were slighter made and who wore simple loose flannel jackets, leaving their limbs perfectly free; and a good use did they make of them, for to their activity and good fielding must be attributed the victory which they obtained. It will be seen by their score that the batting on both sides was by no means equal to the bowling, and that the well-pitched balls of Henry Grace and Ram Chunder Mookerjea made cruel work amongst the wickets. The fielding and general play of Cartick Chunder, Ballims and Hurropersad would be creditable to members of any Mofussil Club, Unfortunately in the return match two of the best Hoogly players were absent and thus an advantage was given to their opponents, which could be ill afforded
I remain
Wicket keeper
Chinsurah December 1856

Hoogly scored 29 in the first innings and 47 in the second and Kishnaghur 41 and 37.

'The Bat', also a keen cricket fan and former player, was not interested in reporting matches like 'Wicket Keeper' was. He was not interested in who displayed more 'bone and sinew' but he indeed was keen to see displays of feminine beauty at the ground.

Being a resident of the French enclave of Chandernagore, 'The Bat' had an eye for French beauties and with the help of French decided to woo them using cricket as the bait. The first two words, 'Being myself and the use of 'fair sex' also gives a hint that he could have been an Indian.

> Sir,
> Being myself an old cricketer and much interested in the game and knowing from experience for enlivening effects of the presence of approving spectators, particularly of the fair sex, I spent a spare half hour this morning writing the enclosed invitation to the Calcutta ladies to patronise the approaching match on the 1st. If you can find a corner for this hasty brochure of a cricketer and thus give *The Englishman's* support to what is essentially the Englishman's game, it may possibly and desirably result in bringing encouragement to the game and bright eyes to inspirit the exertions of…The BAT
> Calcutta, December 22, 1856

The rather long bilingual poem which 'The Bat' composed is interesting in many respects. 'The Bat' would have thought, perhaps rightly, that a combination of French and English would reach his target audience rather than, say, a Bengali-English bilingual effort. We are of course presuming that the writer is Indian but either way it showed fascinating experiments with language that went on in nineteenth-century newspapers. Such poems were frequent, and soon enough we find Englishmen too using Hindi words to embellish their efforts in English. The rhyming patterns are worth a watch.

> *Venez Mes Dammes et Demoisella*
> Really 'tis worth while and well,
> *Si vous aimez jeu, ici*
> Sport in plenty you will see.

Il-y-a des gentil homines
Of whom no doubt you all know some
On, sinon c'est tout le meme!
Who are about to play the game.
Ce jeu, a qui le nom est donne
Of cricket; should the day be sunny
Telle que sans donte in sercrit
Yet not to warm, come see the play
Un jeu si bon, et si joli
We're sure you will be pleased to ace,
Taut de grace, et taut de vie
In Hasleybury's pets you'll see
Tournez las vos eux si leaux
And just observe how matton go,
Voila, vous voyez dans la terre
Wickets three, and bails a pair
Et cette bade, que count si vite
Rolling even to your feet
Avec la bale celle borne ici
Tries to knock off there bails, you see.
Ce jouer done, qui tiet le baton
That 'gent' who has a solar hat on.
Avec le baton fait un coup
With all the skill that he can do,
Et tojours, c'est a dire, s'il plait
He strikes the ball and there-why he.
Avec asset de forde s'il frappe
(This is the luckiest thing that can hap)
Le court, et court, et done il conte
A score for every run, 'tis won
Que dans, un jeu, quelqu' uns personnes
Should count how many each side runs

We are not aware how successful this invite turned out to

be, but a half-hour exertion by 'The Bat' surely provided some entertainment to the readers of *The Englishman*.

There could be a pedant behind these bilingual experiments, but over the years the bilingual osmosis grew beyond all proportions to reach a stage where Hindi words are equally acceptable in English.

Also in verse was a eulogy for Francis Gladwin, who in the wake of *Hicky's* started the *Calcutta Gazette, Asiatick Miscellany, New Asiatick Miscellany* and *Oriental Miscellany,* and thus became the father of periodical journalism, apart from being an Orientalist.

> Merit's gold medal is to Gladwin due.
> Who gave imperial Ackbar to our view,
> His prudent laws, his sentiments on things—
> This living portrait of
> The First of Kings
> Persia thy lore was early Gladwin's care
> The Graces saw—and bade him
> Persevere
> —Hawkesworth

Gladwin was the first professor of Persian at Fort William College. The poet, whose name rhymes with a better-known poet, must have made a deliberate attempt to please this Orientalist professor, but the fact that it passed muster and got published is an indication of how open the language was, even when journalism was taking its first tottering steps in India.

Almost all letters to the editor written during the eighteenth to the twentieth centuries began with an abject prayer to the editor to 'kindly give space'. For instance, 'The Bat' pleaded with the editor of *The Englishman and Military Chronicle:* 'If you can find a corner for the hasty brochure of a cricketer…'

A writer to *Hicky's Gazette* on 18 December 1780 did not plead like normal letter writers do. He gave Hicky permission to print his letter! 'If you think proper to print this, you have permission and perhaps I shall continue my correspondence on another subject.' The publishing of one letter, of course, opened the door to a career in letter-writing.

Another writer prefaced his letter, dated 29 July 1780, professing his love for the pretty wife of a Brit, with a desperate plea:

> Mr Hicky Sir,
> By giving the accompanying lines a place in your nex paper you will oblige
> RLK

It is titled 'A Modern Love Letter' and like the one professing 'higher' emotions for cricket-watching ladies is, in verse, more Hawkesworthian than Wordsworthian.

> I hope you will think it is true
> I deeply am in love with you
> When I allure you the other day
> As I was mufing [musing] on my way
> At thought of you I tumbled down
> Directly into a Deadly Swoon
> An tho 'tis true I'm something better
> Yet I can harldy spell my Letter
> And as the letter you may crew
> I hope you think the form true
> You need not wonder at my flame
> You dropping from the skies
> And let dull idiots fear your Eyes
> With love their flowing inspire
> I tell you they are flame of fire.

Letter-writing as a form, in verse or rhyme, has since the days of *The Englishman,* or *Hicky's Gazette* for that matter, continued to gain popularity among Indian writers of English. To profess love or to complain about the dangers of kerosene oil, people resorted to letters to the editor, a tradition that has taken firm roots.

Many Indian writers opted to write in English to even regional language publications and it was clearly more prestigious to be published in English. Mir Majfar Hussain of Kolkata wrote this letter to the first Assamese paper *Orunodoi* in January 1854:

> To,
> The respected Mr Editor Sir of the newspaper Orunodai Editor sir,
>
> We are very glad at your great endeavour, through *Orunodai,* to bring enlightenment in this country Please oblige us by publishing the following matter in your esteemed daily
>
> It needs no comment about the pitiable condition that our country-men are now living in. But it is a matter of great rejoicement that a scholar named Sir Purnanda Sarma sometimes prints useful things for the good of Assamese people in *Orunodoi* even in such time. But a matter of regret is that these wise sayings of him have been all fruitless. There have been a failure like playing a song before a dead person.
> Sir Mir Majfar Hussain
> Calcutta January 8, 1854

The exact nature of the grouse that Hussain entertains is not clear, considering his sudden departure into an unconnected simile without preparing us for it—or 'setting it up', as we journalists say. The way I figure it, Hussain is suggesting that sane advice given by Sarma about the running of the state of Assam is falling on deaf ears.

The subjects taken up by letter-writers were varied, and on many occasions did not have any sense of purpose or propriety, just eccentricity and the urge to see their names in print. Letter-writers of the twentieth century, like their genetic predecessors, also tried to use pen names and initials. Letters were not just an indication of the changing social and political preferences. Sakina Yusuf Khan reflected this in her introduction to the *Times of India's* collection of Letters to the Editor in its sesquicentennial publication. 'By the beginning of the 20th century we find that the letters column catered to the needs of a more heterogeneous group. The ranks of its contributors had been augmented by the growing class of English-educated Indians. Issues of reform and nationalism were now more important than ever...'

Many Indians took the letter form even further and wrote books in the form of letters. The first Indian book in English was epistolary, written by Dean Mahomed (1759-1851) who wrote letters about his travels and life. 'Through his words, we can see his conception of what being Indian meant, and the implications of that identity in terms of his loyalties and sense of self during this period of the establishment of British colonial rule over India', his biographer Michael H. Fisher writes in *The First Indian Author in English* (OUP). Mahomed's life from subaltern to his settling down in Cork and Bath form an interesting and significant account of Indian life during the eighteenth century. How an ordinary soldier and traveller was transformed into India's first professional writer in English is in itself a fascinating story. The yearning to have English qualities and then to become an Englishman himself, a factor that runs through the Indian encounter with colonial rule, is quite interesting and can be seen most vividly in the well chronicled life of Mahomed.

His letters were pretty straightforward, and when his descriptive powers failed him, Mahomed lifted stuff straight from writers like John Henry Grose *(Voyage to the East Indies—1766)*. But as a subaltern view of things his letters are precious as reportage and thus the first draft of history at a time when few Indians bothered to write anything, let alone such an ambitious series of letters.

The sense of awe in his letters as Mahomed traverses across the subcontinent opens up an unexplored land to the reader. Mahomed's was reportage of the highest order. Nothing missed his eye, nothing was too inferior to find mention in his narrative, nothing too complicated to be left to others to unravel. Since Indians are inured to having their history written by foreigners, Mahomed barely finds mention in Indian historiography and nowhere in Indian academia have I seen his writings slated for study or reading.

Look at the sense of detailing and fascination in his first encounter with Mumbai at a small distance from Surat:

> The English Church at Bombay, is a neat airy building, standing on the Green, a large space of Green, a large space of ground, and pleasantly laid out in walks planted with trees, round which are mostly the houses of English inhabitants. These consist only of ground-floors, after the Roman fashion, with a court-yard before and behind...They are substantially built with stone and lime and whitewashed on the outside, which has a decent appearance but very offensive to the eyes from the glare of the sun...

While Dean Mahomed's life has been well documented through his writings and activities, what is not well known are other epistolary works by Indians which continued the tradition started by Dean. In 1934, Peter Davies Ltd published *Letters of an Indian Judge to an English Gentlewoman*. The judge Arvind Nehra was an Anglophile, and most of his letters were cloyingly sentimental about everything British. So it is no wonder that *The Times,* London, called it 'An extraordinarily vivid and personal account of the life of an Indian educated in England, working in his native country and caught between two cultures'.

Nehra starts out with a typically submissive tone to the English lady for whom he clearly had the hots. The letters have no clear instances of Indian usages but serve to show the Indian fascination for the epistolary form, especially when it came to writing in English.

> You must excuse a letter from somebody you may this morning not even remember. It is the lonely young man with the black face—beside the door—to whom you were so kind last night. I have only just returned from Cambridge to Calcutta and know no one here. It was a real ordeal to find myself at Government House, at such a large party all alone in the world. I was busy wishing the floor would swallow me or that perhaps death would arrive swiftly and quietly when you came over and took pity on me and so turned an evening that began as a nightmare into a very pleasant one for me.
>
> I had intended to call on you this morning, to thank you in person, but I learn that you have left Calcutta for Bombay. Believe me, Yours most sincerely and gratefully, Arvind Nehra

Nehra's letters suggest that the lady replied to him off and on. Her letters are not published, but Nehra's unsolicited letters show his yearning for England: 'standing up there in the sunshine and stillness, I think again of Westminster Abbey which I love very dearly...' The last letter in the collection, which he wrote while waiting for an operation, drips with pathos and some put-on melodrama.

Now it is evening—too dark for me to write to you any more and so for a little while I must say good-bye. The shadows fall, Lady sahib. The shadows fall, I must wait until I hear upon the stairs the feet of one come to light my lamp…

This Indian fascination for the writing of letters—good, bad, literary and indifferent—in English has had a wide-ranging fall-out: the growth of Indian-English. Not everyone had the literary or descriptive powers of Nehra or Dean Mahomed or other early Indian letter-writers. Their ambitions were confined to seeing their letters printed in newspapers and suffixed with their pen names, as we have seen.

Anything could spur a reader to compose a letter in English and send it off to the editor with a desperate plea for inclusion. If cricket was one such early inspiration, on 8 February 1870, Kitty was troubled enough by kerosene oil to dash off this letter to the editor of *Pioneer* in Lucknow. The letter is comic as well as satiric. Kitty, not as well known as other contributors to *Pioneer* like Rudyard Kipling, seems to have been an English lady of some eminence. Her obsession with crockery seems to confirm her British origins, but the use of Hindi words and slang show that Indianisms were becoming contagious.

My Dear Pioneer,
I do so wish you would not go giving people advice without first trying it yourself. You told me in the last hot weather about some wasps with maggots in their tails and when I tried to pick some out I got most dreadfully stung—you old retch! But you made a pretty apology and so I forgave you for once; and now you have actually gone and done me again over that nasty, filthy smelling kerosene. You very calmly and very quietly gave some what I thought, serious advice about oil with blow up what I suppose you call an interesting and

instructive experiment; well I didn't know yon were chaffing, and so when hubby went to kutcherry, I sent for the bearer, and for a match and some oil &c. he poured the oil into one of my best white and gold china tea saucers and I dipped the blazing match in accordance to your directive. Instead of the match being extinguished, as you promised it all went bang! Such a blaze! My pretty saucer is burst all to bits and my poor fingers are burnt so black, and my carpet is in such a mess—oh you shocking deceiver! I will never forgive you this time—no, never, never, never,

Yours angry,

Kitty

P.S. Please send me at once another breakfast set

Such incendiary matters relating to tea pots and other such plots, were to be the subject of missives over the years. Letters were the preferred vehicle for an Indian's first foray into the minefield of English writing. Letters gave the Indian writer the freedom to use Hindi words and Indian expressions, a tradition started in the early letters to the East India Company by its officers here, who did not bother—or could not find—adequate English words to describe the Indian experience. The trend was set in letters written in the early seventeenth century itself. The Hinglish of today got its comeuppance long back by such letters from Richard Baker to Sir Thomas Roe.

Surat, 25 December 1615 (*Letters Received by East India Company from its Servants in the East, Vol. III, 1615*). I quote this to show that the English used in India now has not progressed much.

Right Honourable,

We received your Lordship's letter from Brampoore in answer to a former sent your Lordership and therin understood of your indisposition to health, of which we were right sorry. In the foot of that letter you seemed to be much discontented by means of some information of the disposing of three yards of cloth which Cupid had, wherein we did nothing without the General's orders which was to keep the cloth. We send your lordship's letter to the General for that you wrote you were informed by him that we or some of us thought much that he had that cloth. The General answered that he had wrote nothing upon which any such matter could be collected; and so we desire you to hold a good opinion of us until it be truly demonstrated that we have deserved the contrary.

Touching the governor here we have many conflicts. He hath abused our king in words, for about a month since he asked us by way of interrogation what your Lordship carried up: a drum and a coach and said our king was but as one of the noblemen here, of a little island. So we prayed him to leave talking of princes Matters! Our king was as able to be avenged of his enemies, and better too that the Mogul. This was two days after we received the firman from the Prince; and he told us, when we pressed him with that firman that if we should send for another though he did nothing, yet with the holding up of his finger never a boatman would put his hand to, nor porter to work for us; and in such scornful and reproachful terms: What carried your Ambassador? We have forced to let him take what he will and comes to no account save only 12 clothes' he gives us 15 mahm (udis) percovedoe, but racks so many polling duties—3 pyce out of every mahm (udi) for receiving the money in the house. The cloth was worth 20 mahm per covedoes. Many other thing he hath, both of the company and particular men, which we do not know how to be paid for it and many presents he hath received since your Lordship's departure. Your Lordship in all good service to command
Richard Baker

If parts of this letter read like a modern Indian-English creation, it shows how English has come full circle after four centuries.

This is another letter written by Thomas Mitford to the East India Company written on 8 August 1617 (aboard the *Peppercorn*). Notice the long-winded sentences which are an integral part of Company correspondence in the seventeenth and eighteenth centuries.

> Hononourable and Right worshipful,
>
> My duty remembered etc. the globe and Peppercorn being by the providence of God come within 350 leagues of England, the one from Surrat, the other from bantam with the loss of seven men since their coming from the Indies (for which the Almighty make us ever thankful) of which I purposed in person to have given you the first notice as also to have delivered you all our Indian accounts with certain letter of advice from the prime factors of Surrat, but by reason of sundry difference fallen out aboard the Globe to think it fitter for preventing of all danger to continue heer aboard two or three days after our com[ing] to land until you had notice of our coming and your answer returned; in the mean time thought requisite to dispel these brief lines unto you with a copy of our bill of lading here enclosed to certify of the progress and state of your affairs in the Indian country as also the arrival and departure of your late fleet from Surrat with a touch of Captain Joseph's death in fight with a Portingell carrack...

If there are resonances of such letters in the modern Indian-English letter, it shows how much cliches sanctified by time and tradition cannot easily be wished away. One of the classics of writing in Indian-English is the letter by a train traveller to the authorities of the Indian Railways pleading for the introduction of toilets. Many newsletters and other journals brought out by the Railways contain this masterpiece.

Okhil Chandra Sen wrote this letter to the Sahibganj divisional railway office in 1909. He, like Bankimchandra Chattopadhyay before him, loved the Anglo-Saxon language:

> I am arrive by passenger train Ahmedpur station and my belly is too much swelling with jackfruit. I am therefore went to privy. Just I doing the nuisance that guard making whistle blow for train to go off and I am running with lotah in one hand and dhoti in the next when I am fall over and expose all my shocking to man and female women on platform. This too much bad, if passenger go to make dung that dam guard not wait train five minutes for him. I am therefore pray your honour to make big fine on that guard for public sake. Otherwise I am making big report to the papers.

It is said that it was this letter that resulted in the railway authorities introducing toilets in Indian trains. While the impact of this letter on diarrhoeal passengers might have been heavenly, its effect on Indian-English writing too has had some divine effect: it spurred many others to try to imitate Okhilbabu. The letter does not look like an Okhilbabu composition, for even Bengalis making preliminary attempts at English writing would have done better. The letter looks like someone decided to help out Okhilbabu with some free advice, or he himself was satirizing the standard of English among railway officials. A letter in correct English would not have achieved the desired effect, one can assume. The pathos, imagery and the slapstick elements that the letter conjures up would have sent the divisional manager of Sahibganj in Bihar scurrying to put in place the long-drawn-out process of introducing toilets.

The Railways did not stop at that: it continued to be concerned about cleanliness in toilets in stations and the disposal of excreta. Typical of railway bureaucracy, there have been innumerable letters exchanged on the minutiae of 'nightsoil'. For even the addition of one extra bucket to collect human excreta, the British officials split hairs and argued the matter in many letters and over many months much before Okhilbabu decided to take matters into his own hands.

The railway letters are also classic examples of what I call Gazette English: the language used by officers in the Railways are to this day the guiding light for present-day bureaucrats. The following letters from the East Indian Railway Company Agent's Report, Meeting No. 21 held at Kolkata, 4 May 1876, are good examples.

> Sanitary condition of Cawnpore Station
> The Board hear with much regret of the filthy and unhealthy condition of the Station of Cawnpore which cannot fail to be considered as reflecting discredit of the local officer. Mr Figg's delicate state of health relieves him from much of the responsibility but the attention of the Agency ought to have been drawn at an earlier period to the exigency of the case...

Similar problems were being discussed in other sectors of the East Indian Railway Company. It shows how over the years all attempts were made to keep the Railways clean.

> Conservancy Arrangement at Assensole
> 23rd May 1876
> In returning the enclosure of your letter I beg to submit the following.
> Each house of barrack has an iron receptacle for excreta, each kitchen had an iron bucket for holding dirty water and

a small brick cistern for all refuse, making in all 29 night soil receptacles, including 4 at the station, 99 dirty water buckets and 99 cisterns for refuse.

Letter No. 516 of 4 May 1876 had listed other problems with transporting the human refuse from the stations.

There should be two carts for night soil instead of one as the new spot for trenches is far off. The cartmen now have their cart standing on the road to fetch the refuse and dirty water and sometimes the bullock start on their own accord along drains and fences, damaging the cart which have therefore to be constantly repaired...

Shit work, one might say but the Railways had, in everything they did over the years—from adding new types of seats, to letting drivers go on leave, or advancing money to a driver to bring his girlfriend from England—rules and guidelines that were written and argued over in many letters, and finally resolved.

Petitions to the Railways like that of Okhilbabu, apart from being example of Indian-English, help us to understand how the Railways grew in India and the Indian notions of development and governance.

On 21 August 1881, merchants of Patna city submitted an application to the East Indian Railway Company to build an overbridge in the city. Okhilbabu would have been proud of this application, which reflects some of his concerns about the modesty of passengers:

For the convenience and comforts of the public, the Railway Company have constructed various works for which we should always feel grateful to them. Since the opening of Railways much has been done towards the ease and comforts of passengers of all places, and as we are well convinced that the Railway Company endeavour by every means in their power to afford facilities for traveling by rail, we would beg to state for the information of them that there is a tunnel under the Railway at Bagumpore or Patna city station through which the passenger daily enlighting from the up trains have in order to get the City Roads, to pass with great difficulty and under the following inconveniences:

1st The underfoot bridge is so low that carriages, palanqueens, akhar etc cannot pass at all through it, being about double the height of a man below the rail level and in consequence passengers are obliged to go on foot notwithstanding the sick and the weak requiring conveyances.

2nd There being no passage for carriages and palanqueens, many purdanusheen native ladies alighting from trains are obliged to walk down the place before they get to the road along with other passengers thus reluctantly and disgracefully exposing themselves to the view of the public.

3rd Owing to the path being very narrow at night, the passengers alighting from trains have to push with great difficulty through the crowds and the place becomes so dark that even after 4 o' clock no one is able to go without being guided by light, the weak, the sick and more especially the children of them get hurt when pushing through the crowds.

4th In the rainy season the tunnel is filled with water about 4 feet deep and consequently it becomes impossible when the water drives up the path becomes very muddy and slippery and emits a bad smell which very much affects the health of the passengers as well as that of the neighbouring inhabitants.

We the petitioners therefore beg that the Company be so kind at close-up the present tunnel and build an overbridge similar to that at Dinapur and Bankipure which will obviate the difficulties referred to above and for which we will ever thank the company.

The long-winded petition had its effect. The company resolved to build an overbridge at an estimate of ₹3,060.

Indian officers and staff tried to catch up with their own version of English. If Okhilbabu tried his own version, other railway staff tried their best to be as close as possible to the British version as possible. Interestingly, both Okhilbabu and the merchants of Patna were concerned about the exposures involved. The merchants did not like the women 'disgracefully exposing' themselves, unlike Okhilbabu's 'expose all my shocking to man and female women on platform'.

The language of petitions was sometimes reflected in other memoranda as well. Maybe collective writing was not a good idea. The sudden interjection of big words or complicated usages is a clear instance of the writer taking outside advice or the petitioners deciding collectively on a particular usage after much debate. Note that in all such petitions and adulatory letters the writer sets out to express his linguistic inferiority before going all out in the following paragraphs to make good that deficiency.

When W. J. Littlewood, traffic manager in Howrah, retired in 1919, the staff presented him with a scroll which is now preserved in New Delhi's Rail Museum.

Sir,
With Grateful hearts we desire to express the esteem and admiration we have always borne for you. The feelings of our hearts which deeply regret the loss of your presence from us could scarcely he expressed in language and our hearts are too full of sorrow and anguish to give vent to them.
Yours career has been characterized thoroughly by great

ability, untiring labour, thorough conscientiousness, fostering care and lively tenderness. Your profound knowledge of the Railway Traffic has been an inestimable advantage to your staff and has always guided them in the right direction.

Esteeming as we do qualities of the heart above those of the head, inestimable has been, we must say, your lofty sense of impartiality and justice tempered with sympathy to us.

And now, Sir, in taking leave of you, we earnestly hope and fervently pray to the Almighty that many years of health and strength may yet be vouchsafed to you to work with vigour and renovated energy in the various spheres of usefulness in which you have always moved.

We remain Sir

Your most obedient and loving staff

The word 'move', appropriately for a mode of transport, seems to have been a railway favourite and has been used with various connotations, most of which have been adopted by our bureaucracy and nurtured over the years. So 'to move on the matter' is the metaphorical fall-out of the physical or literal meaning of moving a file from one place to another, from one level to another up the bureaucratic hierarchy. This farewell scroll has brought out yet another usage which could have been popular in those times—and continues to be so in the present as well. 'The various spheres of usefulness in which you have always moved' combines the metaphorical and literal meanings of the word and sees Mr Littlewood as a man with 'renovated energy' who 'moved' from place to place in a hurry.

I read with interest some long-winded, excruciating letters and notings in the files of the Baroda government (Vol. 1, 1905). One, from Dewan J. Manibhai, refers to a new railway line and features again the word 'move', a bureaucratic favourite.

To, Col E.S. Reynolds
Agent to the Governor-General
Baroda,
9 September 1891
Sir,
With reference to the correspondence ending with my letter No 7994 dated 19 June last regarding the proposed Railway from Baroda to Khakharia via Ajwa, I have the honour to state that His Highness Government will be glad to see the work of the line commenced if possible early next season and with this object the preparation of the estimate expedited.

I request therefore in favour of your moving the Railway authorities in view to matters being arranged accordingly as far as practicable.

I have etc.

Manibhai. J

Dewan

Here moving is used to mean 'petition', a popular usage in these days when judges set the tone and rules for everything from municipal functioning to Parliament's duties. On 21 February 1890, the Company Agent in Kolkata received a letter from the loco superintendent concerning a curious matter. Railway authorities spent much time discussing a teetotaller's society and responded favourably to a request to 'move in the matter'.

Mr J. Martin Loco foreman, Dinapore has lately been moving in the matter of starting a Teetotaller's society at that station and has sent me copy of the minutes in which it was resolved to ask you to grant a room free for the first 6 months for the purpose of holding their meeting...

While the railway authorities 'moved' each other and the Dewans asked them to 'move fast', the Gazette gained some words that were to stand it in good stead over the years. This particularly Indian usage has 'moved' far and wide. From a book of hymns quoted in a following chapter is this double whammy which moves 'move' to yet another level. 'Hence inspite of being the great leader of India, Jawaharlal Nehru belonged to the world. We might say he is the hero of the world, one of the very few select great men who moved masses of human beings and who continues to move them.'

Such efforts at letter writing have continued through the years. From Okhilbabu and other railway efforts, I leap across 100 years to bring this letter written by an assistant post master with a proclaimed literary interest, to the news weekly I worked for. He was commenting on the literary column.

17 March, 2005
Dear sir,
This is M Ammasai of Tamil Nadu by name and a reader of…. by identity.
    Your still under 'Take My Word' emits Rays of charm and your article sends X-rays on books and tomes. The book 'Vade-Mecum' is my needy choice. For a long spell it has been on a wild goose-chase. Could you please mind me and mend the torn hope?
    I have been waiting in the wings.
Regards and renewals

This letter too is as much of an Indian-English classic without the diarrhoeal problems that confronted Okhilbabu 125 years ago. A battlefield of metaphors and imagery, it is an indication of how many users of Indian-English are quite ambitious in the way they use words and poetic imagery and how they all summon uncommon usages in the hope that their writing will get due recognition. This postmaster from Bhavani in Tamil

Nadu might have preferred the use of words like 'tome' and 'torn hope' to suggest that he is a well-read man in English, especially since he is writing to a literary columnist.

Ammasai is in search of a book for which he has been on a wild goose chase and in the process has suffered some 'torn hope'. Even the writer Suresh Menon's 'rays of charm' have done nothing to help his shattered hope. However, in the same sentence, when the ray transforms into an X-ray, things take a slightly dangerous turn. The 'ray of charm' is the obligatory flattery which launches many such letters into the literary stratosphere, and the charm here refers to the columnist's photograph. The sign-off offering 'regards and renewals' is not normally seen in Indian-English letters where 'greetings and best wishes to nears and dears' are the common practice. By wishing the writer a renewal, the assistant postmaster may have been wishing him all the best in his weekly writing, a sort of renewal of faith in his profession. Such phrases are not common in letters written in Indian languages, so it is utterly perplexing how sign-offs like 'renewals' find a place as soon as an Indian writes a letter in English.

Humour and eccentricity were commonplace in the letters section of Indian newspapers. But most letters gave advice to politicians on what must be done to help the country progress. The late Girilal Jain, former editor of the *Times of India* wrote: 'Letter-writers practice a kind of journalism, though they are not journalists. They can be interested and partisan; they can be dis-interested and non-partisan; in either case they gave life to a newspaper. It would not be an exaggeration to say that a newspaper is best judged by the quality of its reader's views columns.'

The type of journalism that letter-writers practised consisted of pointing out governmental inefficiency. Letters columns are filled with grouse letters pointing out that government machinery at various levels has reached a comatose stage. From the mofussil to the urban, there is always lax administration, and this has inspired letter-writers over the years. Like this letter from an Orissa town which landed on my desk:

> Dated 16/9/05 Time 11.45
> Subject: complaint against
> Dear Sir,
> I am Santosh from Seniliguda writes you to published the matter very urgent as possible. Here in our town, ie Seniliguda there is much spoiling younger generation ie in panshop sells the beer and wines and brandhy. They is no govt take action about. The younger generation student nevers go to bars and fast food they only go to panshop and have a drink everyday. They is no government takes action about this. Please rectify this and publiced in your paper so that government take action.
> Thank you,
> Yours fathfully

Having taken the trouble to point out that paan shops are selling alcohol, Santosh from Seniliguda also decides to make use of the side margin in the foolscap paper to mention another grouse against which he calls for urgent government action.

> There is a lot of traffic problem in the town ie on Sunday's because that day ie weekly market and no government takes action for removing the weekly market.

The anger and helplessness which prompted Santosh from Seniliguda to pen this petition against local authorities falls in the category of Okhilbabu's letter, the only difference being that Santosh sent it to a faraway newspaper, firmly believing that getting the complaint published is the only way to get the faceless government babu to react. Strangely for such letter writers, Santosh notes down the time of writing, though he leaves us to guess if he is writing it in the morning from office or near midnight after he had a taste of alcohol from the paan shop. Note here that there is an undercurrent of the moral element like in most letters of complaint (younger generation student being corrupted by free availability of 'beers'). In fact, nothing has worried the Indian-English letter-writer more than the corrupting influences of modern life, and most anger is reserved against the creeping canker of modernity. Here, of course, we see Gandhian morality coming to the fore, a quality which most Indians hold dear.

In the evil versus good encounter, few Indians dare take the side of evil and if the perceived 'evil' (alcohol, short skirts and other sartorial influences that young girls are vulnerable to, bribery topping the list) shows signs of winning over the good, divine and moral, immediate recourse is taken to letter-writing. Such letters always made it a point to score a double hit: one against moral erosion and the other against the perennially inefficient government, like Santosh here has done. Bur nowhere is the writer bothered about getting help from a more experienced English letter-writer, for he believes that the language he uses is the language that must be understood by the masses.

The importance of letters in the evolution of an Indian form of English expression has been important. Letters columns were also the first trial of your prowess in the arena of both English and current affairs. Experienced and well-known writers used the section to lampoon and lambast, like this extremely funny letter written, I believe, by A. E. S. Talyarkan, legendary sports commentator, who signed this letter in *The Times* self-effacingly with just his initials. It was a way of smirking at Indian-English conversation as well as a snooty swipe at the emerging social mores of the day.

It is dated 10 June 1942, and does not throw light on the immediate provocation for the letter, though it seems AFST was perturbed by the engaged tones that Bombay telephones were often stuck with.

> Sir,
>
> Here is why Bombay's telephone subscribers use the telephone four times as often as New Yorkers. First and frequently: 'This is me darling! Tired? Coffee stall—eleven thirty—cheerybye'.
>
> Secondly and more frequently: 'Who? Oh, hello! I say, did you see that tripe in the papers this morning—yes—no—one thirty—rightiho.'
>
> Thirdly and oftener: 'Pesi? Dolly! Cocktail dance? Club-rum my-Albless. Bang—Tummy—daktar—ispital uthamna—three thirty—sahebjee!'
>
> 'Fourthly and always: 'un, allow?...en allow!...allow! array Changanlal? Allow?...array Maganlal?—allow—arey bhai, allow? allow! mundi—aha?—allow? Dana; chokha—opening—closing—doogo—tigho—allow? allow? hajar?—urdho dippher vaicho—allow? allow bolo!'
>
> And baloney! Let's have the message rate!—AFST

AFST was taking a dig at the Indian way of handling phone calls. Once a house gets a connection, it is assumed that along with the instrument come a few stock words in English which the user would have to master. So the proud telephone owner—now, the cellphone user—starts off with the 'allow, ellow,' and then progresses swiftly to 'Espeak to Maganlal pleejj' but soon enough he discards the English terminology and gets down to the familiar terrain before winding up the conversation with a flourish: 'Ok boss, hangover *kar raha hoon!*'

This letter clearly supports Jain's views that, in a way, letter writers were citizen-journalists, holding up a mirror to society. The fact that Talyarkan wrote letters to the editor was news to me, but this could have been his formative phase in which he was trying out his writing skills, to be the hallmark of sports journalism in years to come.

The perplexing question about why many Indians turn to English when they want a document has been discussed earlier. Though weakness in English and the use of Indian-English cut across class barriers, it is a common misconception to attribute the use and propagation of Indian-English to people from the lower classes or those who are neo-literate. The increasingly large number of tribals converted to Christianity, the neo-converts, are thus largely unfairly supposed to be purveyors of Indian-English. It is assumed by many that neo-converts cannot speak proper English, though I have heard tribal priests speak excellent English.

So the converted tribal—straitjacketed in a cultural limbo—is a sitting duck for caricaturists and humour writers. Enos Ekka, an independent tribal MLA in Jharkhand, became the target of this satire written by my former colleague Pamela Philippose of the *Indian Express,* who in keeping with this common Indian perception, labelled Ekka a practitioner of Indian-English and then went on to tear him apart in her weekly humour column. The formation of the government in the state of Jharkhand in 2004 depended on his vote and Ekka had made known his support to Arjun Munda of the right-wing BJP. So, in every sense, Ekka becomes a target. Look at his perceived profile: poor tribal, taken over, acquired and merged by marauding missionaries in the tribal belt of Jharkhand. He picked up bits and pieces of English from Jesuit schools, but did not quite manage to learn English well. Politics is his choice of profession and not preaching from the pulpit. And now he stands a chance to make some money to prop up a government which needs his vote. If another MLA in a similar political situation were an upper-caste Brahmin who had taken a similar decision to support a BJP government, he would not have been ridiculed like this.

The default social category of the English speaker in India is the brahmanical elite and the 'power' sects, all of whom would at some stage have studied in missionary schools. Ekka too may have passed through the system, but the effort of tribal leaders like him to be counted among the elite (though he has managed to become part of the ruling party) are constantly thwarted. A tribal with the chance to change the fortunes of a state or control ministry formation, is perceived as a man too big for his boots, and so he becomes the right candidate to be squirted with some smelly ink.

Pamela's satire is an explanatory letter by Ekka, though there is no salutation. Ekka describes what has been happening to him of late. Note the funny spellings, Hindi words and other classic Indian-English expressions. The style is clearly epistolary and the column is a good send-up, though it sometimes degenerates into cheap caricaturing and social labelling. So Ekka is shown as a man who even does not know what a helicopter is.

> You are seeing Jharkhand mamla on TV no? Like in Hindi fillum, there is car chases, helicopter rides, hiding and seeking, suspense, drama…all fillum things. Arrey baba, what to say, I am too excited only. Arjun Munda saab is now Chief Minister and, myself, Enos Ekka am minister. See we are ikyalees, 41, peepuls who are with Munda saab through thickness and thinness in this mamla. But who is chief hero? Just be taking one guess. Yes it is myself Enos Ekka, now minister. Previously

nobody was knowing this humble MLA from Kolebira. Now the whole India is knowing my name. They are asking, 'Who is Ekka?' Then they are asking even more, 'Where is Ekka?' They are sending polis to finding me. TV is capturing my photo and everytime everybody is wanting to know who I am supporting.'

Arrey baba, I am saying no, that I am with Arjun Munda saab. I am telling and telling. 'I am with NDA'. But no one is believing only. They are still asking. I am still telling. Arrey baba, this is simple mamla. See, between yourself and myself I am telling. Munda Saab is more promising that Soren Saab. Arrey baba, Munda saab is always promising and promising and I am trusting his promising. I am trusting because he even sent helicopter to Koleibra for purpose of taking me to Ranchi. Arrey baba, that was too thrilling only. Whirr, whirr, *hawai udaan* came down from skies, just like in Hindi fillum, and then came lifting me up to the clouds like that hero fellow, Akshay Kumarji. And then he is making me minister. What he is saying he is doing.

The long satire in Indian-English ends with Ekka asking his readers to watch him on television being sworn in as minister.

Anyway, you will be watching me being minister on TV. I am too exited only. Myself, Enos Ekka, Hero No 1, Minister and your humble Aaj ka MLA.

There is always this uppity effort to link language and class. The aristocracy and the upper class are not expected to speak like Enos Ekka and God forbid if any humour columnist points out misplaced syntax and Indianized usage to anyone from that class. Good English and superior class are not just mutually complementary in India but also mutually compulsory.

About a year later, Ekka struck again. He along with a few other legislators switched sides and decided to support a candidate favoured by the UPA. Sure enough, humour columnist Pamela too struck in her column dated 17 September 2006. That easy target had popped up again and it was time to swat him down and in the process give the column some laugh lines. Using almost the same opening lines as her column a year back, Pamela, lambasted Ekka again for his presumed misuse of English. The subtext was again emphasized: those who spoke Indian-English had no moral scruples and were thus unfit for any political role.

> You must he following Jharkhand mamla on TV and newspaper, no? How four brave ministers of NDA, Munda government took matters into their own fingers and removed CM kursi from under Arjun Mundaji. Down he is falling. Now please don't be misunderstanding us. Mundaji is no doubt good man also. We will always be remembering him for giving us good time in Jaipur last year when we were supporting him. My mouth is watering when I think of sumptuous Rajasthan CMji gave to us last time—cake and pani puri and what not—such nice-nice shows, such nice-nice sights…

The column gains confidence as it progresses and ends with a libellous suggestion that the money he received for the political favour would be safe in Swiss bank accounts:

> I am also learning that there are good-good banks in Switzerland which is also very useful *chees* for any extra cash flow…

The caricatured Indian-English user draws heavily on Hindi, not just to point to his deficiency of English vocabulary but also as a not-too-subtle pointer to his roots and unEnglish upbringing.

I put this proposition to author and social anthropologist Sanjay Srivastava of Deakin University, Melbourne, and the Delhi-based Institute of Economic Growth. He seemed to agree. 'There is no doubt a link between English and class, as well as English and class aspirations. So, for example, those who absolutely refuse to speak to their children in anything but in English in public are those whose family background is Hindi-speaking (speaking for North India). I have often come across parents answering their children in English when the child clearly speaks to them in Hindi at home (and looks at the parent with puzzlement and incomprehension). In this case, English is also linked to a transitional class: those who are moving from one kind of cultural sphere to another. Those with a longer history of English in their family are quite comfortable with using non-English languages in public. The transitional class is in the process of establishing its metropolitan middle-classness. I think the other aspect to it is that it is increasingly difficult to establish class difference through earlier markers of class, such as clothing. So, almost anyone can now dress in jeans and T-shirts. Hence, speaking English becomes another layer of the Indian politics of distinction and differentiation.'

Knowledge of 'proper' English has for long been a social marker. It is to this need that 'English-medium' schools catered. To be finally pronounced as the parents of English-speaking children would mean that the parents had made one quantum jump in the social hierarchy. So it also gives rise to a situation peculiar to India: the children are uppity and English-speaking and thus part of the elite, and the modest parents with their Hindi or Tamil feet firmly planted in another social milieu. A cultural gap adds to the generation gap, creating a social maelstrom at home. This is similar to the situation which happens when children return from abroad and are unable to connect with the family's linguistic or social norms.

English was the passport every Indian craved for and this suited the purpose of the British admirably well. Not surprisingly, this intention is made evident in one of the early issues of the first Indian newspaper, the *Hicky's Bengal Gazette or the Original Calcutta General Advertiser,* which began its shortlived and cataclysmic existence in 1780. Tucked away in a single column in the issue of 24 February 1781 is this notice inserted by Benjamin Whitehead. His name is the heading too [note that Hicky used 'f' in place of 's', quite possibly since he did not have enough of 's' types]:

> Who formerly kept a School in Calcutta, takes this method of acquainting the Public, that he has lately returned from Habeeb Gunje, with an intention of going to Europe but having been disappointed he has taken a place in the Country, agreeably situated in a good air, on the right hand side of the great Road, beyond Chitpore Bridge...where he propofes Keeping an English Boarding School for young Gentlemen, where Youth may be Boarded, lodged and educated in Reading, Writing and Arithmetick and taught in a plain, eafy and expeditious manner to speak and write English correctly on the following terms...

Global experts of the language too have linked knowledge of correct English to social status. David Crystal in *The Stories of English* says that the notion of correctness in the use of English came only in the late eighteenth century when self-appointed grammarians and lexicographers emerged. William Deresiewicz of Yale University, writing on the evolution of English in the *New York Times* (9 January 2005), says that behind the linguistic anxiety lay an anxiety about status. He backed up Crystal's views about status and the English language in eighteenth-century England. 'Commercial expansion, imperial conquest and industrial revolution were creating a vast new middle class. Just as a host of conduct manuals had sprung up to teach these socially insecure "new men" how to act and dress, so did the language pundits step forth to teach them how to speak… Correct English was upper class English.'

Eighteenth-century England is now being replicated in India in an eerie replay of social history. The rapidly transforming lower classes, powered by the engine rooms of education and political empowerment, are demanding and getting their share of jobs and national wealth. With that comes the need to speak and know English, an effect so well captured (as often happens) by the title of a Hindi movie: *Raju Ban Gaya Gentleman* (Raju becomes a gentleman). To thus get the label of being a gentleman with all its attendant elitist perks is the mantra of every Indian. Indian-English is one of the rungs they must perforce ascend to reach that pinnacle of donning the gentleman's tailcoat and spewing the socially accepted form of English. The title here also has the subliminal suggestion of an underprivileged person who works his way up and then with a final heave-ho finds himself sprawled on the mosaic floors of the middle class, craving for acceptance.

As a symbol of arrival, the knowledge of English has few parallels in India. It is the gleaming new Mercedes on the porch of the arriviste, it is the armour against snide attacks by snobs (view Pamela's column) who arrived earlier and made themselves comfortable in the nicely feathered nests of social achievement.

Gandhi himself had to undergo this transformation and he worked hard towards it, considering he was a bad student in school and terrible at spellings. Sunil Khilnani commented on

Gandhi's transformation which was later to be echoed by our cinematic Raju, though the circumstances and the aims were different. 'In London while learning the law, Gandhi set to the task of making himself an English gentleman. For this, a confident grasp of the language was essential. In his early months he felt acutely his weakness in this respect. To master his fear, he decided to take elocution lessons—his teacher "recommended Bell's *Standard Elocutionist* as the text book, which I purchased. As I began with a speech of Pitt's..." It was through these first, hesitant steps in impersonation that he was ultimately to find his own voice.'

His early form of writing which Khilnani quotes was 'arch English': 'Amidst thoughts, I came unconsciously in contact with a carriage. I received some injury. Yet I did not take the help of anybody in walking,' Gandhi wrote about his journey in England.

Such fear of English and the urge to conquer it can be seen in many of India's great writers. R. K. Narayan himself studied in a school where Tamil and Sanskrit were mocked at. This was the case with many Christian schools, so the shame of speaking in Indian languages was borne by many generations of Indians and was an accepted burden for Indian students for long, and continues even now. From that shame came the inspiration to master English. For, before spending long hours trying to master English there had to be a complete rejection of the local language, either in terms of future professional use or even for social stature. The English schools provide the impetus and environment for that. The craze for 'English-medium' schools is as much a craze to shrug off everything local and Indian. Considering the many years of anti-Indian subliminal propaganda, it is amazing how Hindi and many such Indian languages stood their ground and grew—as spoken languages, if not languages of professional use.

In George Orwell's *Burmese Days,* when the Burmese butler at the club shows an unacceptable proficiency in English ('I find it very difficult to keep ice cool now') he is rebuked by the white sahib. 'Don't talk like that, damn you—I find it very difficult! Have you swallowed a dictionary? "Please, master can't keeping ice cool." That's how you ought to talk. We shall have to sack this fellow if he gets to talk English too well.'

Raju after becoming a gentleman thus faces the wrath of the gentlemen at the club. Orwell's observation can have chilling resonances in high class society too, where the memsahib is bound to stifle the educated son of the housemaid if he ever dares to ask for a favour in English. *'Tu* dictionary *khake aya, kya'* could be the memsahib's response echoing that of Orwell's white sahib. So after having achieved the power of English it is also necessary to keep others from being too proficient in it. The early forms of pidgin English could have been suggested to the butler by the sahib himself who must have loathed the day the Indian butler or servant asked him: 'By the way, aren't you going to the hills this summer?' The sahib would have much preferred that the servant ask him, 'Sahib you no going to hilly place?'

The early English letters written from India can be seen to have left their imprint on the minds of Indians, for some of that phraseology persists in Indian-English after having been debunked by proponents of correct English and banished to the periphery—from where those who were trying to gain entry into the realm of English picked them up. The language's link with status is frightening, in a way. What it means is that a man cannot live in a slum in India and yet know correct English.

This could be seen as a colonial legacy. Knowing of English was for a long time linked to decent social status and good behaviour. The *Gazette of India* has this entry regarding an election petition in 1953: 'He is a fairly educated man and knows English...'

To know English is to embrace affluence itself and shrug off the disgusting stick-ons of a Hindi or a Sanskrit past. To bring out this Indian dilemma, G. C. Bhandari from Meerut resorted to poetry like many others we have seen in this chapter. He sent in his poem to Khushwant Singh, who found it funny, ironic and incisive enough to reproduce in his widely-read column 'With Malice Towards One and All', in *Hindustan Times* in late 2006.

> Can you speak English, my ambitious boy?
> UK for you is then a land of joy
> Go to a temple and ring its bell
> Learn out to perform its rituals well
> Knowledge of Sanskrit will not click
> Unless you pick up the tongue of Tom and Dick
> Britons don't allow such priests to sneak
> As they cannot freely in English speak
> You may not be a Pandit or a tilakdhari
> Fluency in English can make you a trained pujari!

Ironically, English continued to draw on local factors and usages despite this continuing emphasis on correct English. The concept of correctness itself is a late entrant. The dictionary and forms of etiquette were developed as social markers, while English grew so fast because it refused to be segmented or corrected or remain the voice of a particular social segment. So we see the incorrect forms being sucked into the acceptable form, out of necessity. 'If you can't beat 'em, join 'em' seems to be the presiding philosophy. Many see the vernacular and broken English as harbingers of change and growth. Deresiewicz writes:

> Nonstandard varieties—the language's blood, muscle and nerves—are equally valuable. They are English with its ear to

the ground, the language as it is lived; the vernaculars of the kitchen and the street of youth culture and ethnic culture. They are also the enduring wellsprings of literary achievement. The genius of English is an oral one, its literature greatest when hewing closest to speech (Chaucer, Wordsworth, Dickens, Joyce). It is no accident that our greatest author was a playwright. Anyone who fails to hear in the language of rap the harbinger of a new chapter in our literature's glorious history has a tin ear and a tiny heart. I don't mean children should not be taught to speak Standard English. I do mean they should learn to value their own vernacular as something more than 'broken English'.

Despite all this, there is a lingering anxiety about linguistic misuse. It worries English users immensely, it makes them smirk and laugh and run down the user of corrupted English. Different versions and usages of Hindi are, for instance, accepted as dialects or regional variations, but never scoffed at or given social tags. With English it is another matter.

In his *Outlines of the History of English* (University Press, Cambridge, 1900), T. M. Toller wrote this preface full of foresight:

> For to realize the language of a people at any time in their history would be to realize their life at that time; it is in the words that their thoughts remain embodied, and really to understand their words we must feel as they felt. To follow a language completely throughout its gradual development would be to follow all phrases in the changing life of those who spoke it; and only as the powers of the imagination are cultivated in progress made towards this ideal. A language gain may be regarded as a living organism, ever undergoing changes of which some, though they may be vital, yet do not affect its outward form, for words may keep their form but

change their meaning; while others are visible, for words may
be lost or gained or re-shaped or re-arranged...

Jug Suraiya, in his long career in the *Times of India,*
caricatured Indian-English with rib-tickling effect. In occasional
middles and his column, Suraiya was the supreme caricaturist
of Indian follies and pronunciation and the gleeful announcer
of the latest Indian-English coinage. Indian usages often bring
out the loudest guttural laughs from English newspaper readers
in their elite salons. Critics of Indian-English like to consider
themselves the educated elite (a qualification that requires the
understanding and articulation of correct English), though no
Indian can claim to be free of the regional language influences
that swirl round him all the time. So annual editions of the OUP
dictionary are always the right subject for edit page treatment,
as a third editorial or a middle, and there has been no one better
than Jug for that self-deprecatory take. As an observer of Indian
idiosyncaries and caricaturist, Jug has few parallels in modern
journalism.

On 2 May 2005, Jug wrote this bylined article in his favourite
epistolary style, from an Indian-English user of the Oxford
dictionary. The occasion for such pieces, which comes when a
revised OUP edition is published with new Indian usages and
words, is a cause for celebration and opinions are expressed
about how Indians are now rightly striking back at the empire.
Supplying them with more and more words, you know!

In his usual style, Jug does not hold back any punches. The
article is also an exposé of Indian-Hnglish as we know it with
hype and a bit of his fertile creative mind used to good effect—
addressed to the OUP editor. The Hindi slang, the Hinglish
creation, the Indian phraseology and the rustic touch are all
there. Jug's humour is popular because he makes his comic takes

appeal to a pan-Indian audience, and his Indian-English brings
in argot popular in regions from Kolkata to Ranchi to Haldwani
to Ludhiana and, of course, Chennai. Note that nowhere does
a caricatured Indian-English speaker sound apologetic about his
choice of words but in keeping with the pattern tries to introduce
new phrases. Strangely enough, and not just coincidentally,
classic Indian-English letters have references to private parts and
'expose all my shocking' like Okhilbabu did.

> My head is eating circles and circles over all this *golmal* about
> new Oxford University Press (OUP) Advanced Learner's
> Dictionary having Indlish (ie Indian-English) wording-From
> A For ABCD (American Born Confused Desi) to Z for
> zulm (cruel treatment ie. Police doing zulm by giving danda
> to publics committing nuisances in frontside of mantrijis
> dwelling abode in capital)—we are using in our daily to daily
> gup-shup. One auntyji, whose good name and hailing from
> what native place I am not knowing but putting up at my
> backside itself, is telling that it is a very shame-shame business
> which will make us laughing joke of whole world as because
> of our khichri way of speaking. Just I am saying her, please
> not to take it otherwise but what it goes of your worthy father
> if all outside people learning our *bhasha* which even if I am
> telling myself is too good only.
>
> We are not needing OUP dictionary to be knowing that all
> such talks are not bogus *lafra* but simply way we are speaking
> from Kapurthala to Kanyakumari, ay-ay-yo. Loin in Punjab
> is not private part which decent gentry not mentioning in
> front of convent educated ladies and small baba-log but big
> animal first putting up in jungle and now in cage in joo where
> people paying money to come and see it. Any gujarati snake
> is not kingcobra, not even on Narendra Modi, but just it is
> time-pass like *ghatia*.

And suchlike that all Patelbhais are having between morning tiffin and nightly dal-bhat. Outside gentry not having inside khabar on loins and 'snakes' and *joos* was getting too much shocked and *gabhrooed* and telling that India is most third class and hopeless place full of rascal people that is best avoid *karo*.

As first to first attempt to show outside world how we are speaking, OUP dictionary deserves shabashi. Tourist people and foreign sethijis and moneybags will now be knowing that India is number one locality for making holiday or doing dhandha-baazi without any khit-pit or gich-mich. But while OUP is giving many good dialogues of local people like 'Don't take your grandfather's time to do your homework'—no doubt very fine dialogue which with my own ears I am hearing first time only—it is not telling anything about grandfather's better half i.e nani as in 'I will make you remember your nani' most famous dialogue popularized by late Rajiv Gandhi who another one time also told *'Hum losenge ya jeetenge'*. Also OUP is mentioning chargesheet but not CBI, hawala scam etc which are leading dialogues of India today.

OUP editor, kindly to ensure correction of all such omissions, commissions and kickbacks. And how it is that OUP is telling that it is dictionary of 'Current English' when whole brother-in-law world, ie *puri Sali duniya,* is knowing that current English is same to same as current Hindustani except letterings are in Roman script, not Devnagri? Please to be doing needful. *Bahut shukriya aur hazar* thanks.

This abiding concern about 'public committing nuisance' in front of mantriji's house or inside the railway station cuts through centuries, as we have seen from Okhilbabu's letter to the Railways. Everywhere this national concern about shitting, pissing and disposal of other excreta has been a sort of national shame which is not expressed in public debate but written out in Indian-English. If the administration anywhere wants to admonish the public, preach civic cleanliness and other concepts alien to Indians, there is always a sudden summoning of English. This habit has also provided Indian-English a shitty metier. Public notices and admonitions are seldom issued in Indian languages. Is this because of a feeling that it is outsiders, tourists especially, who have no concern or care for the cleanliness of the place, unlike the locals who try their best not to dirty their own backyards?

I traced this national habit to the extreme points of India. Near the Mawsmai limestone caves near Cherrapunji in Meghalaya was this board:

> Warning: Excretion, urination, throwing rubbish or doing immoral act inside the sacred forest is strictly prohibited. Anyone who violate will be punished as per village law. By order: Sirdar, Mawsmai.

This, of course, was an effective warning because I too was looking for a place to 'violate' and do some 'urination' when I was confronted with this board. I decided it is much better to piss in my pants than find myself at the mercy of the village law, the details of which were not announced anywhere, not definitely in the Constitution of India. In the northeast, tribal law prevails in many parts and the village sardar is all-powerful. I imagined being hung upside down near the mouth of the cave, which is the most frightful place I have entered, and that too after paying for it. Being inside the cave with your feet on the ground was frightening enough, for I felt like a mixture of Neanderthal man and Indiana Jones.

What if the village council decided to sentence me to one week under one of the giant trees with only rice-brew to sustain me? Nothing could have been worse. The rice brew which people in Cherrapunji and nearby drank instead of water was the most tasteless and eeky beverage I have ever tasted. The brew apparently takes you back to the past, and tales of history and legend come swimming into view. This I realized after my taxi driver stopped at a tea-shop for a surprising half-hour and came back with a smile and a stink. He started telling me tales of Cherrapunji's past. That convinced me he had read my book *Under a Cloud,* and after that I was friendly with him. But when he, a Nepali migrant who had lived in Shillong all his life, started relating myths from the Middle Ages, I realized what he had been up to in the old lady's shop.

In fact, I even gave up the very idea of committing an immoral act, which was to buy a bottle of Bacardi Breezer which an old lady was selling in her shop along with Pepsi and assorted chips—and also, surprisingly, dried mushroom, the only link the place seemed to have with the forests which skirted it...

Morality and other such concerns are then a driver of Indian-English. If romance drove the great writers to higher realms, morality drove many to plumb the depths of language. The best example I was able to lay my hands on was a short-lived Delhi rag called *Sunday Diary.* The copy I have is an assassination special, considering how many characters it mounted an attack on, apart, of course, from the language. The weekly newsmagazine was distributed free and the cover story informs us 'Public feared About Bomb Blast'.

Sunday Diary had discovered a new form of investigative journalism, which was to publish the bio-data of their target, saving its staff the trouble of conducting any investigation. The issue had the curriculum vitae of two people, one a union minister and the other the owner of a south Indian chain of hotels, the latter convicted for murder. His bio-data reads:

Character: He is always kept other person's wife for examples 'kruthika', 'jeeva Jothi'

Habits: He is a Womaniser

Wors Character: he wants beautiful girls and other persons wives only. He spends a lot of money to separate the husband from his 'target' lady and then he marries her. (Kiruthika's husband got diverse & by this way). Not only married ladies but also young girls, he doesn't hesitate to kill the wanted ladies husbands

Close friend: Sexual doctor Mr…and some other doctors. They give Harmon injections and other medicine to him.

The magazine obviously has mastered the art of writing a CV, considering they investigate 'wors characters' as well. The profile of the Union minister from Tamil Nadu also gives investigative journalism a new edge. The magazine could also predict what would happen, as this bio-data shows:

Policy: Looted 25 % of amount which has allotted for national plans, and saves it by his benamies.

To be happened: shortly Income Tax department will raid all the…. department.

Property: Earned 1000 crores by looting the allotment amout of the government.

Habit: head Weight and always changing in the character only time of elections he will give respect to superiorministers…

Sunday Diary, however, had its morals right. An invitation to journalists to apply for jobs in the organization had to be accompanied by this declaration:

I solemnly consent to work as a Reporter/Photographer for a period of one year in the Magazines, published on behalf of the

Association. I accept to receive th stifne [stipend?] and I will never claim for salary. After a year, if you or your association wish myself to appoint as a Full/Part time employment, I consent for the same with concluded Salary.

With this concluded summary I rest my case.

6

LOOKING TO GANDHI AND NEHRU

> How we wonder with what miraculous talent your
> Inner Voice absorbed the leaves of the Voice of the
> World! Where you not blessed with the Sixth Sense
> as the ancient Indian Rishis were? A perfect man
> of action you were. No wonder, you had the most
> Rare Sense in abundance. What an extra-ordinary
> Transmitter!
> —Hymn in praise of Nehru, 1982

The English versus local languages debate continues, though in the search for global positioning Indians no longer want to be seen as a Hindi-speaking nation, like the Japanese are clearly a Japanese-speaking nation. English, in fact, is now considered a national asset, even though there still remains a government department for the spread of Hindi, which tries to translate official documents into Hindi and issues occasional exhortations asking bureaucrats to embrace the native tongue, hoping they wouldn't take such commands seriously.

The debate was national in nature—and was accompanied by a national dilemma. The south of India embraced English heartily, and the north took to Hindi naturally. Over time, there has evolved an implicit understanding on the issue, leading to a dual stream of languages. The dilemma was real, like we saw in the case of Zaka Ullah. Mahatma Gandhi too was unhappy with the use of English, but like many Indians he resorted to the language when it came to writing, though he mostly spoke in Hindi. According to R. Parthasarathy, who wrote *History of Journalism in India, From Earlier Time to the Present Day* (Sterling), 'Gandhi was not happy editing an English weekly. He was forced to do it. He did it as a concession to the non-Hindi south' and said:

> I frankly confess that to me editing a newspaper in English is no pleasure. I feel that in occupying myself with that work I am not making the best use of my time. And but for the Madras Presidency, I should now leave the work of editing *Young India*…The English journals touch but the fringes of India's population. Until Hindustani becomes compulsory in our schools as a second language, educated India, especially in the Madras Presidency, must be addressed in English.

R. Parthasarthy paid glowing tributes to Gandhi's writing style:

> Gandhi's style was simple but effective. He used simple words and short sentences to drive his message home. He chose his words with precision and there was no ambiguity or confusion in what he wrote. He opened out his heart and shared his inner most thoughts and feelings with his reader which evoked an emotional response…His compassion, humility, nobility and his concern for the poorest of the poor breathed through his writings.

The problem started when others tried to breathe Gandhi's style into their writings. Gandhi's attitude towards English was ambiguous. He struggled hard to make his own English simple and lucid and gave no concession to frills. For him, his English writing was the big tool that he used in building up the national movement. It helped all the more considering that he was not the best of orators. He, like Nehru, could inspire through his writings. He could use English to his advantage while not recommending it wholeheartedly for the masses.

'To give millions a knowledge of English is to enslave them. The foundation that Macaulay laid of education has enslaved us. A universal language for India should be Hindi,' Gandhi wrote in *Hind Swaraj*. 'His opposition was not to English but to what it symbolized: political slavery and cultural degradation,' according to Arvind Krishna Mehrotra. At various times, Gandhi especially had warned of the dangers involved in taking to English. But ironically for both Gandhi and Nehru, English was an instrument to subjugate the empire rather than a language that enslaved them. Both of them resolved this paradox to their own benefit.

Gandhi did not discourage serious writers from taking to English, just as he did not discourage himself, despite his fear of the eventual outcome if the language was popularized beyond a certain limit. His view, expressed at another time, was that the best language for communication should be chosen. When Mulk Raj Anand sought Gandhi's opinion on whether it would be appropriate to write exclusively in English, he replied: 'The purpose of writing is to communicate, isn't it? If so, say your say in any language that comes to hand.' Once he even asked Anand to simplify his language.

This is the Great Indian Paradox that confronts users of English in India. The way out is the Gandhian way: express your misgivings about the language and continue to use it. It is a dilemma that faces established writers and aspiring writers as well. Established writers have this conundrum to confront: is English adequate to capture Indian experiences? Indian writers over the years have answered this question convincingly, smelting the language in the throbbing heat of their febrile imaginations: giving words meanings they never had, yanking out words from Indian languages and making them fit their narratives, and finally remodelling the vehicle to carry the great Indian story throughout the world.

Even while the importance of English was being debated in English and other Indian languages, people merrily invented their own form, which goes by the name of Indian-English, the acquisition of which was the quarter-way mark in every Indian's journey to become a 'gentleman'.

The English writings of Gandhi and Nehru were huge influences in India. If both of them had chosen to do all their writing in Hindi, in keeping with Gandhi's initial views that English was the language of slavery, then English would not have acquired the required legitimacy and the great ripple effect which saw it emerge as the working language, the elitist language and the language of governance (though not the language of the masses). The Gandhi-Nehru stamp of approval was a must for the people. Apart from inadvertently influencing and inspiring many Indians to take to writing novels (many of them classics), books and theses touching on Gandhi and Nehru, these two giants of the Indian consciousness also set English on its path to glory in India. One reason could be the enormous amount of literature that the national movement produced. That in itself made a tremendous impact.

The major reasons for the creation of a throbbing and growing subgenre of English can be traced back to how Gandhi and Nehru inspired the people. Many of those who used their inadequate skills in the language to publicize, criticize, moralize and issue clarion calls to the people were convinced that they were playing a stellar role in the national movement. Such books form a subgenre by their startling naivete, constant hugging of the superlative, convoluted, misplaced imagery and metaphor, total indifference to accepted norms, the self-adulatory tone, and of course profoundly prosaic arguments. Underlying this is the faith of the writer that in creating such a booklet or thesis in English, he had accomplished the impossible, and having done that, deserved a place in the racks reserved for timeless classics.

Another reason for the plethora of clumsy Indian-English tomes on Nehru and Gandhi or those inspired by them could have been that publishing houses thought that the subject matter would find a captive audience. The Indian Printing Works of Lahore was among those small publishing houses which had a laundry list of such books, advertised proudly in all its publications. When it was not *Nehru: The Humanist,* it was *Nehru: The Leader of East and West,* and if no other aspect of Nehru readily presented itself to the publisher, out came a book called *Nehru: The Man.* All these, while paying their respects to Nehru or Gandhi, blissfully forgot to pay homage to the language in which they wrote.

A large number of people took up writing in English in a bid to encourage, support and then be part of the entire paraphernalia and groundswell of the freedom movement. Some used the subject and the language with the limited, egoistic objective of seeing their works in print. Some wrote to defend Nehru against attacks by critics, others wrote glowing hagiographies to both Gandhi and Nehru. Others just wanted to put their praise on record and hopefully get noticed by the powers-that-be.

'Several years ago I read D. F. Karaka's book *The Lotus Eaters of Kashmir.* The book at places left a bad taste in mouth and the author in sum-total was less than fair to Jawaharlal Nehru. Ram Manohar Lohia in his book *Guilty Men of India's Partition* was more than unfair to Nehru. A study of these books prompted me to attempt in this small volume an assessment of Nehru's personality or an exhaustive knowledge of the literature available...' L. N. Sarin wrote in his eponymous book in 1968 (S. Chand and Co.) justifying his writing of the tome.

Not only did Indians learn a lot of their English from Nehru and Gandhi, they also used English—or their own version of the language—to join in the national discourse, or so they believed. The use of English by these two intellectual giants in communicating to the country triggered off an avalanche of interest in the language and also an intense longing to join the club. During the freedom movement and after, there was a deluge of English in the form of pamphlets, monographs, critical theories and the like. Reverential, aspiring writers taking their first hesitant steps in a foreign language milieu summoned the spirits of Gandhi and Nehru to guide them or at least asked for their blessings. Many others were inspired enough to write their own books on national problems in English, an indication of how much influence Gandhi and Nehru's English writings wielded on the Indian linguistic consciousness. These were of course writers who remain unknown and unsung, quite apart from major writers like Mulk Raj Anand, Raja Rao and R. K. Narayan, who used Gandhism and Gandhi himself in their English novels.

Apart from English, there is quite a large body of novels in Indian languages which picked up the political philosophy of Gandhi and Nehru—but our concern here is just the undercurrent of that national stream or the subgenre that was the byproduct of this nationalistic outpouring. This showed the yearning among those unqualified or not talented enough to adopt the language of communication of Nehru and Gandhi and thus identify with them and their cause completely—intellectually and linguistically.

Hussain Khan, BA, BT (Bachelor of Art, Bachelor of Training), teacher at the Government Training College for Men, Mysore, was among those who were inspired enough to pen monographs on these Indian leaders. Hussain did not have much critical acumen and his booklets are a marvel of Indian-English. Like many of his ilk, when he fumbled for words, he filled up his text with cliches and inanities. Needless to say, language was the victim. In *Immortal Men,* he bravely ventured forth to hold aloft the twin flags of nationalism and English. But I am not too sure whether it gave any coherence to the ultimate object of all this writing. Judge for yourself:

Jawaharlal Nehru would ever shine as one of the twilightest stars in the firmament of human race because he had in himself the priceless virtue of soldierly spirit combined with statesmanship. It would suffice without contradiction to imortalise his name, to carve out his living picture in the hearts of ours and to accord him a place in the world with the great benefactors of humanity.

Both of them (Gandhi, Nehru) like two facets of the same coin acted and reacted in company with others with the then prevailing situations in India. Then they chalked out a programme a formula or a charter of human rights on the basis of human dignity and humility, thinking themselves neither superior nor inferior to any one, just to lift up those fallen in a ditch of degradation. For its early realization Gandhiji had evolved an inspiring dream of life, so to say, when the throbbing space with teeming millions were readily waiting for its extraction or impression and when variedly required colours were available for its painting with the exception of an apt artist. It was at that hour of need, Jawaharlal Nehru offered himself as much to fill up the gap and to drag out as completely as possible the soul-elevating vision of his master's heart for public enlightenment.

Further as an expert would touch the imagination of onlookers in the game of cricket with gaiety, daring and sacrifice Jawaharlal Nehru effected the same in the political sphere of his time. And again as the perfectly adapt and chiseled batsman who would stand unmoved as the bowler approached the wicket and remained unmoved as the ball was delivered. Jawaharlal Nehru accomplished his task in the like manner.

... Therefore it would be quite possible to think that the people who have showered tributes upon him and also generations might certainly draw inspiration from his ennobling traits: his charming speeches, his immortal lore, his love to peasants and crowds his fancy for nature's things...

Hence inspite of being the great leader of India, Jawaharlal Nehru belonged to the world. We might say he is the hero of the world, one of the very few select great men who moved masses of human beings and who continues to move them.

An unflappable and irrepressible writer, like other practitioners of this genre—as we shall see—Hussain has also written three other books or booklets in English: *Pandit Nehru: The Jewel of the World*, *The Eternal Flame of India* and *Dr Radhakrishnan and his Message to Mankind*. Hussain will hopefully be considered as the 'twilightest star' in the firmament of Indian-English.

The dependence on superlatives, the frequent summoning of divine and cosmic imagery, the search for epic phraseology, bizarre allegories, similes and metaphors are tried and tested Indian-English tactics. Nothing short of painting the subject as the greatest, biggest, tallest will do. In all such efforts, the hero or subject of the treatise is invariably compared to the stars or a person whose name holds universal sway ('jewel of the world', 'hero of the world' and 'voice of the world'). The ambition of the writer invariably raced far ahead of his understanding of the language. Khan's attempt to bring in cricketing metaphor is unusual, and the fact that the metaphor falls flat is no surprise, since the use of any such literary technique is beyond the capabilities of such writers. In any case, no batsman will remain stationary or 'unmoved' after the ball has been delivered. Unless it is Virendra Sehwag fitted out with an advance missile warning system.

Khan, at least, did not try to link cricket to Nehru's philosophy, like Professor J. C. Sharma, MA, did. The learned professor took an instance from an actual cricket match that Nehru played. With a pole-vault of his imagination, he yoked it to Nehru's diplomatic prowess. In *Nehru: The Humanist* (Gandhi Memorial Trust, Gurdaspur, 20 paise) Sharma wrote:

> Mr Jai Singh Member of Parliament once organized a cricket match to help the flood victims in Andhra and Punjab. Mr Nehru led one team, Dr Radhakrishnan led the other. In this match Panditji took a very difficult catch at point, the batsman being Keshav Dev Malaviya. Later, when he was batting he had as his partner the communist leader A.K. Goipalan and made three runs not out. This was a living example of his doctrine of 'peaceful coexistence'.

Sharma forgot to mention whether AKG was a left-handed batsman as well. Who knows if the grounds for the deft leftward movement of the Congress in later years and its garlanding of socialist mores were laid in such cricket matches in which communist leaders confidently batted left-handed? One hilarious instance of the garnering of superlatives can be seen in Jagat S. Bright's booklet *Jawaharlal Nehru: A Biographical Study* (Indian Printing Works, Lahore, 1945). A caption accompanying a picture of Nehru in a Fedora did what many words could not: 'Every inch a statesman! From beneath the shades of his felt hat, the eyes of Jawaharlal glint like a rapier into the devildom of Western diplomacy.' In his introduction to the book, Bright goes a bit incendiary with adjectives and over-the-top metaphors:

> The career of Pandit Jawaharlal Nehru has been an embodiment of 'Service above Self'. His has been a statesmanship of selflessness and self-sacrifice. He remains unfaded and unfading in the whirling bursting world in which we live today. Pandit Nehru is a live figure when the very notion of the abiding seems a myth. He is a scholar, a patriot, a lover of truth, an unflinching opponent of whatsoever things are debasing. He has given his life to the country. His devotion to internationalism has lent to him an added glory. His ideas and ideals like the snows of the Himalayas, convert themselves into the melted floods which fertilise the globe.

B. N. Ahuja, MA, JD, also from Lahore, can give Bright, resident of the same city, a run for his money—at least when it comes to gathering superlatives and collectively dumping them at Nehru's door. In his foreword to *Jawahar Lal Nehru: The Leader of East and West* (Varma Publishing Company, Lahore) Ahuja wrote:

> Pandit Jawaharlal Nehru stands next only to Gandhiji in leading the struggle of India for freedom. Whether a young rebel or a consummate statesman he is the Man of Destiny in Modern India. Dynamic and daring, fearless and forceful he

is by common consent one of the most fascinating figures of
the 20th century. In him Indian patriotism and nationalism
have reached their highest watermark.

Reaching high watermarks is the least of the achievements
of writers of Indian-English. The problem starts when they
confront their characters in swimming pools and then go on to
figure out where the high and low watermarks are. J. S. Bright,
in yet another effort, *The Great Nehrus,* got around this problem
by converting the entire watery scenario into an extended
metaphor. His book looked at Motilal Nehru, Jawaharlal and
Vijayalakshmi Pandit, all related to each other. In a chapter
called 'The Lord of Luxury' he builds up the aristocratic image
of Motilal as he lounged in the pool in Anand Bhawan, though
he did not know swimming. In the process, the Indian National
Congress became a swimming pool and so the stature of Motilal
Nehru or Jawaharlal Nehru automatically reached the high
watermark, though Bright measured nationalism in 15 inches
of water.

In the evening the friends of Motilal used to come to the pool.
The house and the pool were fitted with electric light. One was
a novelty the other was an innovation. The pool was swarmed
with bathing parties. One of the distinguished men of today,
Sir Tej Bahadur Sapru was a frequent visitor to the pool. He
was then a junior at the Allahabad bar. Neither Motilal nor
Tej Bahadur knew swimming; but while the latter sat on the
first step in fifteen inches of water refusing absolutely to go
forward even to the second step and shouting loudly if anyone
tried to move him, the former could manage to do the length
of the pool with set teeth and violent and exhausting effort.
This difference in the physical character was later on illustrated
in the political outlook. Sir Tej Bahadur Sapru throughout

his life has remained a liberal sitting on the first step of the Indian National Congress in fifteen inches of nationalism and absolutely refusing to move forward even to the second step of non-violent non cooperation and shouting loudly if any one tried to drag him into the extremist fold. On the other hand Motilal Nehru crossed the entire swimming pool of the Indian National Congress, with set teeth and violent effort which transformed him overnight from an extreme loyalist to the extreme nationalist on the right hand of Mahatma Gandhi. Sir Tej has remained an admirer of Mahatma Gandhi only from the other side of the swimming pool.

Practitioners of this subgenre wore their degrees on their sleeves, or rather on the (book) jacket. Hussain's BA, BT is matched by H. Dhand's MA and the BA (Oxon.) of S. Saleem or the MA of Jagat S. Bright. The announcement of academic qualifications was part of the author's effort to lay claim to the right to hold forth in English. This would not have been essential in a Malayalam or Marathi book, since the writers had a natural claim on the language. Hence a BA (Oxon.) writer was meant to be a much better writer in English than, say, Hussain's BA, BT. Here none of the writers are from the fringes of society, nor are they clawing their way back into the mainstream after being flung away by cruel fate. They are mostly from the higher castes and, more important, well educated. If English was not part of their curriculum or their daily interactions, they had no reason to feel guilty about it. But they all did. And then they had the higher calling of connecting with the freedom movement.

H. Dhand's tribute to Nehru appears in a collection called *Jawaharlal Nehru: Apostle of Peace*. The interplay of extreme forms of praise and high-sounding divine imagery is frenetic. And like his contemporary Indian-English writers, Dhand, MA, did not make use of his critical faculty when writing such eulogies and thus added nothing to our understanding of Indian history, if at all that was the aim of his article. The intention was, of course, to drown Nehru in superlatives, and this called for the suspension of the critical faculty.

> Millions of Indians thought of him as Father Jawaharlal. Others referred to him as 'chacha' (uncle) Nehru. Whether they called him father or uncle, Jawaharlal Nehru, was the living idol of his countrymen.
>
> His prestige had gone far beyond India's border. With his *achkan* (long coat) his Gandhi cap and a rose in his buttonhole, Nehru a product of seven years of uppercrust English schooling was always a familiar sight at the gathering of world leaders. Nehru was people's pride and people are India's pride—and problem. The nation's more than 450 million faces all have mouths to feed and eyes that looked questioningly for what the future might bring to a land mixed with automobile factories and wooden plows, jet aircrafts and crossbows.

Even with such daunting diversity, Nehru was a catchword. 'Intelligent conversation is becoming very dull,' observed a Delhi socialite. 'You either start with art critics and end with Nehru or you just start with Nehru and end with Nehru.'

The last paragraph of Dhand's article expectedly serves the avowed pan-Indian aim of placing Nehru on the Great Indian Pedestal by terming him the largest personality in India: often irritable and quick to anger, sometimes impatient with criticism, recipient of the reverence of millions yet modest and humble, a man whose private pleasures tended towards 'mountains, running waters, children, glaciers, good conversation, all animals except bats and centipedes'.

Nehru and Gandhi were bestowed equal rank by the average

Indian. There would have been protocol problems if one tried to position them in order of importance on the Indian pantheon. Professor Sharma got around the problem of weighing the relative greatness of Nehru and Gandhi by the simple expedient of counting the number of people who died of shock at the death of each of these leaders and how many days the nation shut itself down for mourning:

> Mr Nehru had ingratiated himself so much with his people that at the time of his death a good number of persons died of shock; many fainted, the innumerable people felt as if they had become orphans. The voluntary hartal was observed for two days. At Gandhi's death there was a single day's 'hartal'. A few people had fainted but death out of shock were not many. We may account for this phenomenon by declaring that while Gandhi was worshipped by the people, Nehru was loved by them.

Sharma has here judged Nehru as higher up in the immortality stakes, but in another book, *Mahatma Gandhi and Nehru,* he restores parity and says:

> It will not be very wrong if the history of India is summed up in the name of Mahatma Gandhi and Prime Minister Nehru since 1916. Both of them were great men and their greatness was mainly responsible for weathering the storm. For when one looks back over this period of our history or look into the future one finds it a very difficult period—a period full of difficulties, hazards and turmoil. This period saw a great country emerge from the most inhuman and dismal condition to most honourable and human conditions of life. The process to-day seems simple, peaceful and easy, For all this transition, no human blood was shed as compared to the history of modern China or USSR. In short, greatness

has been achieved through real peaceful means and India has become a progressive country.

All this is due to two men who dominated the scene. The two great actors had acted their part so well that this colossal drama came to a glorious end or beginning!

Why did the use of metaphors and similes fox all these writers? Why is it that professors Sharma and Bright, who could have read all the masters of English, remained blissfully ignorant of what could be termed as primary equipment in a writer's repertoire? The reason obviously is that all of them took to English writing inspired by Nehru/Gandhi and not because they were equipped to do it.

And why did they not have that crucial self-doubt? Forget about self-doubt, such professor-writers believed that they were breaking new ground. Bright, in his introduction to the *Nehru: A Biographical Study,* sought to draw a distinction between biography and biographical study and pitched his book as belonging to the second category: he asserted that his book was definitely a biographical study. The plain and simple biography, of course, was left to lesser writers to handle.

> A biography is not the same thing as a biographical study. The former is objective rather than subjective. A biography may be only the narrative of a hero; a biographical study—if a study at all—has to be more or less critical and psychological in its attitude towards the hero. It may be a critical appreciation. And mine is definitely one.

By proclaiming its superiority and emphasizing a new genre to which his work belongs, such writers were only trying to underscore their importance in the debate. Desperate attempts were made by writers of Indian-English to get an angle to work on. The fact that Nehru and Gandhi themselves wrote on various topics made the task of finding new angles difficult. In search for an unknown angle, Bhopal Singh wrote *Nehru: The Artist* (Gandhi Memorial Trust, Gurdaspur, 20 paise) and went on a tangential approach to the subject. Of course, he had his own thesis on dog-eared books. He did not possess a copy of Nehru's autobiography but that did not stop him from writing on the subject after borrowing the book.

> Recently I borrowed a copy of Nehru's Autobiography from a library and found that it was so generously thumbed and dirty that for a moment I hesitated to touch it on purely hygienic grounds. Incidentally, I suggest that it would be in the interest of public health if there were a regular medical inspection of all libraries so that books rendered unclean and dirty by readers' thumbs could be periodically destroyed. And yet, second thoughts suggest that these books may be retained. The clean or unclean appearance of a book is an index to the favour it enjoys. The same criterion applies to part of the same book. It occurred to me that to know Nehru's attitude towards beauty in life and nature, I should find out the cleanest pages in the book. That was so. I found that the cleanest pages in the book described Nehru the artist while the most thumbed pages were a record of Nehru, the politician.

Having expressed his desire to read only clean pages (as opposed to writing clean copy, I guess), Bhopal Singh set about the task of discovering the artist in Nehru and established at the very outset that:

> Nehru is an artist in a word. He loves beautiful phrases and creates them without effort. His prose often rises to the level of literature and possess a force and vitality which is the outcome of sincerety…

More recently, a Nehruite published not a novel or a poem but hymns in praise of Nehru in English. *Our Dear Nehru,* published in 1982 by Ravi and Rahul Book house, from the Trivandrum suburb of Kariavattom, seems to be an effort to gain some political mileage, since the booklet has a letter of recommendation from the Congress leader the late K. Karunakaran and G. Karthikeyan. The intention of having chief ministers or politicians write recommendations is also a well-worn strategy to get funding from the party or government for the publication of the book. It could also serve as an application for getting a party ticket for an election, though here it does not seem likely.

But why English? The reason is clear: to get noticed by people who matter and to put forward your claim to be part of an imagined national pantheon of writers who have critically appraised the two giants. Thus you contribute your mite to nation-building.

Writing in English had other advantages. The magnum opus could be offered to a 'world-wide circle of readers', as L. S. Seshagiri Rao wrote in his introduction to the translation of the Kannada book on Kamala Nehru by K. S. Ratna Rao (Bharata-Bharati Pustaka Sampade, Bangalore ₹1.50). 'These books were first written in Kannada. We are glad and proud to offer them to a world-wide circle of readers. Welcome to the world of greatness', Seshagiri Rao wrote. That was the intention of all such writers.

English books reached all libraries, like Pillai's hymn for Nehru. Having printed 1,000 copies, Pillai made it a point to send a copy to the Nehru Memorial Library in New Delhi with a neat calligraphy-style petition written on the first page to the librarian, pleading for it to be placed on library shelves. There it stands today, adorned with layers of dust pointing to its neglect, squeezing itself in among the mighty tomes of Nehruana, its slight and humble presence ignored through the years as scholars turned the pages of the big volumes that held more secrets of nation-building than a book of hymns.

Varkala Sivan Pillai had a lot of books in Malayalam to his credit, but he obviously felt that his oeuvre would not be complete without something written in English. One thousand copies of *Our Dear Nehru* (*15 Hymns*) was published in 1982. Pillai made his intention clear in the preface:

> This collection of 15 hymns 'Our Dear Nehru' is my eleventh work in English, throwing light on the universal personality of Jawaharlal Nehru. I have tried to depict his many sided greatness and have also tried to evaluate the unique Indian leader from various angles. Indeed, I have done it as a creative writer.

Pillai rounds off the preface with: 'There are only very few men of the ages in history who can stand on a par with Nehru. This is a very humble work on such an immortal Indian.' The preface does not claim that the author has studied any unknown facet of Nehru or Gandhi, and so he cannot be accused of being pompous. Chapter heads are named 'Tree' and 'Bird' and written in paragraphs and not rhyming lines (too much of a bother for Pillai, I would guess) with most sentences ending with an exclamation mark rather than the normal full-stop, suggesting that the author was quite impressed with his own poetic prose. The Indian-English writer, as we can see, had a totally different perspective on the aesthetic, the construction and even the notion of a tribute to a leader.

Chapter 1: A tree
The Jewel of the World sprouted on the canal-bank fertile, as cultures ancient all sprang from the soil stream-soaked. The seedling grew into tree lovely and shady, it broke leaf into,

all was a flame with joy, millions of blossoms it bore, lakhs of fruits it held, bliss it bestowed on crores.

How you won the brilliance of world fame, how you endured the most arduous forms of tasks, how you let not evil fortune fall upon us, how we failed to find a better stronghold or fortress. The wish and will, zest for life and the quest for truth we got in plenty. The countless hands wave and warn the world. Your charming presence! How can we help but love our Mother India!

You were far, you were near, you were high, you were low, you stood still, you shook from trunk to top.

Millions consumed with fire of grief found shelter under you, many a hopeless heart sought solace leaning on your safe trunk.

Here it is difficult to figure out if Pillai is addressing Nehru or his motherland. Most likely the lines are directly addressed to Nehru. The following lines are clearer.

You are as immmportal [!] as the papal tree pictured in the Indus seal, you are as immortal as the papal tree in Kurukshetra, you are as immortal as the pipal tree in Gaya, you are as immortal as the Indian Puranic Kalpavrksha, you are as immortal as the Christmas Tree, you are as fruitful as the *coromandal* coconuts, you are as valuable as the Indian trees of spices, you are as Universal as the tree of Universe, you are as divine as the tree of knowledge, you are as permanent as the tree of Supreme Bliss.

The Wind of Time blew over the Indian green fields took rest in the vast estates, slept in the thick forests, stayed on mountain tops, drank from the sweet Indian rivers, *bathed* from the Indian Ocean, prayed in the holy temples, visited the tourist centres embraced the big Indian minds and the big Indian hearts, kissed the sweat-bathed Indians, wandered with the pilgrims of clouds, sang with the sweet birds, warned the unkind, praised the kind, howled with the beasts, whistled with the machines, argued with the politicians, played with children, lunched with the Indian artists and Scientists, kicked the unpatriotic, saluted the patriotic, cursed the war-mongers, blessed the peace-makers.

It murmured at your ears; What a wonderful Indian tree you are!

Pillai, like many proud and unhindered practitioners of Indian-English, throws caution to the winds, with the result that metaphors get a real pasting! Summoning words from the classics (Kurukshetra, *kalpavrksha*) and imagery which sounds poetic (Wind of Time), Pillai raced forward. He was never parsimonious in showering praise. Other Nehruvites may, however, find fault with him for comparing the leader to Coromandel coconuts, rather than Kerala coconuts, which are fleshier and sweeter. The alliterative effect must have forced Pillai to go in search of Coromandel coconuts instead of sticking to home terrain. Having exhausted all possible classical and poetic imagery linked to trees, Pillai, in what can be called natural progression, starts comparing Nehru to birds. But if we think that exclamation marks might—like his 'Wind of Time'—be given a 'rest in the vast estates' or be allowed to sleep 'in the thick forests', then the reader is bound to be a bit dismayed. Yes, and Nehru is the Bird of Humanism. Better than being the Crow of Socialism.

Chapter II: Birds

The Bird of Humanism! How you cool, how you burn, how you madden, how you enliven, how you enrich the hearts with the sweet songs of Humanism! All tongues fail to tell what a balm it is for the sick and hungry hearts. Herald of

Modern India! How aptly you know the truth—heart, mind, thought and body are interlinked!

Warm our little hearts with the life-giving warmth of your Big heart, fill out little hearts with the sweetness of your Big Heart. The extreme joy over-flowed from the heart and made others joyful as well. Indians never had such celestial joy again. For Indians all, super Joy is all.

You flew up, you flew down, for days you were tongue-tied, for days you sang, for days you twittered. Rejoicing and *torturing* you met, the fire and shower you witnessed, days and nights you *befriended* with, the world you made your family, the people you made the members. For them you showered the nectar, dreamed, laboured, planned and lived.

The power is in the thing that runs all in, it is the same power all is made of. Knowing it well you worked for the well-being of all.

For the first time in the book Pillai refers to Nehru as the herald of modern India. But in the course of the second chapter Pillai makes the bird Nehru move around a bit for he 'flew up, flew down for days you sang, for days you twittered', an exercise which could leave even any giant, let alone the giant of the Indian state, utterly exhausted. In yet another characteristic leap, Pillai gives words meanings which are exactly opposite to what they mean in accepted English. For instance, Nehru is tongue-tied, but sings and twitters for days. Pillai, like many other Indian users of the language, would have surmised that tongue-tied means that the tongue is too busy singing and twittering.

After exhausting all possible metaphors, similes and imageries and having satisfactorily and let's say successfully pasted Nehru on the national template, Pillai in the last chapter, on page 44 of his book of hymns now summons, with a last-gasp effort, a modern metaphor and compares Nehru to 'the voice of the World'.

Having seen that Pillai had announced that Nehru is the Voice of the World, I presumed that Nehru would be compared to a radio. Sure enough, in the second sentence, Nehru is called the All World Radio, dismissing the Indian version All India Radio, with all its flaws, as unworthy. Pillai is careful to continue with the radio metaphor and the word transmitter is predictably used. Having been a transmitter it would be ideal to let Nehru have a receiver as well, and so towards the end he is given 'an inner receiver'.

XIII
The Voice of the World

The Voice of the World! 'The All World Radio;, the Universal Feeler! 'The Heart of the World!' The growing Universal Mind! Speak for the whole world. That lovelier expressive voice! How alien are stiffness, dryness and woodenness to it!

Voice the voice of the first Voice! Let us feel the First Voice through the voice. There is nothing but the voice. Your voice is the sweet form of the first Voice. All is the Voice.

The Ocean meets the waves and the ripples, the Abode of water meets the tiny drops. The Sun meets the rays, the Father meets his dear children, the creator meets his Creatures, the Tree meets its offshoot, the powerhouse meets the light, the Star meets the planets, the Solid meets the gas, the Mother Atom meets the little atoms, the Life meets the little living beings.

The All powerful voice sits on the back of the brave bearer, the All pervading Air. How eagerly the Almighty, embraces His beloved Offspring.

Your tongue was deep-rooted in the sweet spring of Humanism, the tongue pouted the melodious songs for the heart of the world.

The Inner Voice was tempered and forged in the Holy-Fire Indian, the tongue was trained in a country foreign. The mind glowed for a peaceful world, burned the human hearts, refreshed the minds, widened their outlook, showered a new light led them forward, shared their pain and pleasure, dived deep into the problems Universal.

How rich you are with valour and integrity! Never false-hearted towards the world. How you teach all should be of good cheer.

In the world of politics, the name of our Dear political Architect, stands on a par with the names of Abraham Lincoln, Lenin, Col Nazar, Chou-en-Lai, *Churchill* and Marshall Tito.

How we wonder with what miraculous talent your Inner Voice absorbed the waves of the Voice of the World! Where you not blessed with the Sixth Sense as the ancient Indian Rishis were? A perfect man of action you were. No wonder, you had the most Rare Sense in abundance. What an extra-ordinary Transmitter!

Having conferred Nehru with such powers, Pillai ends his tribute, satisfied that he has done his bit as a Nehruvite. Since Nehru has become a transmitter, Pillai's help, I guess, can be dispensed with.

Not all those unknown people who paid tributes to Nehru were practitioners of Indian-English. Non-resident Indians too wrote tomes. *Nehru: Champion of Peace* is one of those tomes written to 'help young men and women of India in the study of the life of Jawaharlal Nehru and of his achievements during the period of his Premiership of India', says S. Devdas, who proudly announced that he was a non-resident by putting '(of Burma)' after his name on the cover.

Others were not satisfied with writing such eulogies alone

and took giant steps to write the big novel in English. By writing a novel in English the author I am quoting next believed that he was carrying forward the noble tasks set for the nation by Nehru. S. Saleem, BA (Oxon.), apparently a police officer who seems to have known Nehru, perhaps having served as part of his security entourage, wrote a crime thriller in English in 1953, with the unlikely and long-winded title *MUDLY: A Romance of the Hills and Hotels (Exploits of a Police Official)*. It was printed and published at The Searchlight Press in Patna and those who wanted copies could contact the Patna address of the writer, suggesting it was self-published.

Mudly is the name of the police officer protagonist in the novel who deals with the criminal underworld and spends a lot of time with a beautiful lady, appropriately named Pretty, who seems to be some sort of double agent.

> To Jawaharlal Nehru
> This book is dedicated to Shri Jawaharlal Nehru in memory of several months spent together in Switzerland in the year 1926-27.

On the next page is the letter to Nehru. The informal tone of the salutation suggests that Saleem had more than passing acquaintance with Nehru, or it would have been addressed to 'Shri Pandit Jawaharlalji' or even 'Respected Nehruji'.

> My dear Nehru,
> I hope you would find time to read this book, if only to see how fiction has solved the problem of financial ills of our country. I would feel amply rewarded if I know that these pages have provided you even with a half-hour of relaxation.
> Yours sincerely
> S. Saleem Mayfair, Fraser Road, Patna

The fact that almost all the books by Nehru and Gandhi are compulsory reading in schools and colleges explains how their works have impacted thousands of Indians who use and want to write English. Their role in encouraging, legitimizing and inspiring English use is as momentous as the other acknowledged roles they played.

> Each in their own way had shown, by their distinctive uses of English, the infinite adaptability of the language of the colonizers. And as they did so, they shattered the belief that Indians were less 'natural' users of the language—so undermining yet another foundational pillar of the Empire. By devising for their own purposes a language that could be deployed across a variety of arenas—law courts, public meetings, pamphlets, newspapers, autobiographies and histories, private letters and constitutional drafts—they gave Indians a formidable weapon with which to challenge the British. But perhaps even more remarkably Gandhi and Nehru gave their countrymen the possibility of an equal conversation with their conquerors.

Thus wrote author and academic Sunil Khilnani in an essay in *The Illustrated History of English Literature in India.*

Those who followed in the footsteps of Gandhi and Nehru were not commercial-minded and may not have hoped to rake it in, but were confident that their books were marching towards the destiny of immortality.

I was surprised to discover that K. A. Abbas, well-known writer, used Indian-English in an imagined letter to Mahatma Gandhi written by a child. His intention was of course to capture the poignancy of Gandhi's death and Partition, but the very fact that he resorted to a letter replete with spelling mistakes and well-known Indian-English usage, shows how prevalent and acceptable the form was. Abbas's intention would also have been to reach out to a section of those who would not have understood his 'correct' English. It also shows how much Gandhi as a person dominated the thinking of the country's intellectuals.

Letar Fraum a Child to Mahatma Gandhi can be found in a 1952 collection of Abbas's articles called *Cages of Freedom* (Hind Kitabs Ltd, Mumbai). The letter, in turn cute, evocative, and poignant, is an attempt to take a different perspective on independence and Partition. The narrator, of course, did not belong to the English-speaking elite but still chooses a language which he is not comfortable with. This was part of a national malaise which Abbas would have wanted to point to or even satirize—such was the tug of English and more so the parallel form of the language on the Indian subconscious. The letter is a boy's-eye view of Partition and Hindu-Muslim tension and so gives us a totally different perspective on things. It is not an imposing story, nor is it history from the heights, it is the real story, a subaltern version of events.

To,
Mahatma Gandhi Saheb,
c/o Gaud Olmaity,
Haven
Bapu!
I am not myself alone riting this letar but others are making me rite it. Those who are making me rite are as falous: My yunger brother Bundoo (whose real name is Banday Ali) my elder sister Zenab and yunger sister Sakina, our naybours son Gopal and Gopal's yunger sister Seeta. And yes, Mohan, a little refooji boy from Panjab who lives near us. I almost had forgot him. You see he aulso wants me to rite to you but he has sed it not with his tung, but with his eyes. He does not say anything with his tung. He speaks only throo his eyes. His

eyes speak much but I will tell you about them after. At this time I only want to say that Mohans eyes are also saying rite to Bapu. So I am writing this letar. Please axkuse me. Wont you Bapu.

Note that the child is aware of his low stature as a letter-writer and thus starts out with an apology and a petition for 'axkuse'. And, in keeping with the pattern, the user of the Indian form of English forges ahead—having apologized once, he does not see the necessity to rein himself him in throughout the discourse.

You are a grate man. You must be thinking why the child's riting letar to me. But we hear you like childs very much. In one foto I saw you sitting and lafing with childs. Gopal says he saw you one time on Juhu beech when he seez your foto his eyes wich are always so sad looking become brite with happiness and say he is our bapu why should we fear him. If you will axkuse me I will say that in your lafing foto you luk just like child or baby who has no teeth even like Gopals smol brother who also drinks goats milk just like you.

My name is Anwar Ali. But everyone calls me Annu. My fathers name is Akbar Ali. I am eight year old. My mothers name is Fatma but everyone call her Fatto (she is not fat but Fatto is amo for Fatma): her mother also lives with us. Grandmother is very very old and all white hair and no teeth. (Just like you!) This our hole family axsept my sisters Zainab and Sakina.

My father did not lie you. He sed Gandhi is enemy of Muslims. Mother sed what father sed. But grandmother she says Gandhi is Gaud's man and he see everyone like brother. Father says grandmother is too old so cannot understand difikult work of politiks. Father is much ejucated at Alligarh collij and read paper every day so we believed him not grandmother. So when talk was about you we sed bad things about you and lafed also bekos you luked so funy with your naked body and loincloths.

One day we heard India was to be cut in two pieces like grandfathers property after his death half came to father and half went to uncle. One day I asked father what is Pakistan. He said it will be country of Muslims own, where we will have our own raj. I was very happy to hear this bekos I na a poper of colour fotos I once saw foto of one raja all in gold and silver cloths and waring daimands and perls in nek. So I sed when we Muslim have our onw raj we will all hekum rajas and were gold and silver cloths and daimons and perls in our neks. And we shouted Pakistan Zindabad, Pakistan Zindabad!

Then after Pakistan was made we herd Hindus beating Muslim every were. That is what my father who read paper sed. So we were angry and hated Hindus. But one thing I did not understand. Muslim were many in sum places like Panjan Fruntier Sind—why they not beating beating and killing Hindus who were few. Perhaps they were doing it olrite but father sed no only Hindus bad and making trouble for Muslims. After ol I am child. So I kept quait and sed nothing before father but in my hart I thout much.

Now I want to tel you about my gun. It is very beyutiful and nise and makes big nois. My Father gave it me on my fifth birthday saying I must play with gun and bekum soljar of Pakistan, it is reely only playing a gun but all childs fear it and with it I Paraid my Pakistani Fauj of childs which contens my sisters and other.

In house next to us there is Hindu Sena of gopal. Oll childs is like us. Gopals father is rich baniya merchant like oll Hindus that is what father says. Gopals unkel very strong Hindu and paraids in Shwaji park with Hindu Sangh army. The oll hate Muslim and Gopal paraids his Hindu Sena Every day. But they have no gun like mine only tin pistel and bow and arros of bamboo. They shouts Har har Mahadev and

Hindu raj banaengay. They also shouts other Hinds crys. They are ten twelve childs and we only four childs but we not afred. We brave Muslims and we have gun after all. We fite them when the come. When they shouts Har Har mahadev we shouts more Allah O Akbar when they shouts Hindu Raj Hindu Raj we shouts Pakistan Zindabad. We live in shwaji Park with Hindus olround. Father says we not to shout like that or Hindus will kill us. Grandmother also tells not to but we not afred. One day gopals army attack us so we fite and they run away when I also sho them gun. But Bundoo fall down fearing Gopals pistal.

When we were fiting I saw Mohan for fust time. He was sitting on boundri woll luking at our fite with strange eyes like he had seen such fite before and not like it. When I went near him I saw he crying with tears but not speaking only luking with those stranje eyes. I once saw a mad fakir his eyes were just like this. So I thout this also sum mad child or may be dumb so cannot speak. Then Gopal came and sed don't teese Mohan he pore refooji boy from Panjan whose father killed and so he now staying with relashuns. I felt very sory and did not injoy playing with gun. At nite I saw in bad dreems Mohans stranje eyes lurking at me and I cried in sleep and mother sed there there, take name of Allah seven times and devils will not truble you. I took name of Allah seven times abut devils trubled me oll nite.

Mohan alwez sat on boundri woll and saw our play with those stranje mad eyes. He played not with us nor with Gopal only sat quait thinking Gaud nows what. And madness increased in his eyes and we wondered what they had seen that he had bekum like that.

We herd on radio you were fasting unless Hindus of Delhi bekum olrite with Muslims. When she herd it teers came in grandmothers eyes and she did not eat for one hole day and even father sed if there is one good man in Hindus he is

Gandhi. Trying to copy grandmother I also fasted one time but before evening I was in bad condishun and my hart was not in play or school work but only in fud and oll time I think of pulao and shami kababs. And I think how you can fast for such long time and not eat anything.

When you were fasting for many days and we had in hole country Hindus and Muslims were saying they were sory for beating and killing each other and swaring hefore you they will not fire now we also stoped play of Hindu Sena and Pakistani Fauj.

At play time we all siting quait and not playing when Gopal comes and says Hello annu.

I sed hello Gopal and what is the talk.

He sed Bapuji and started crying with teers.

That day radio sed you were very week and sick and cannot sppek even so thinking of that I also began weeping.

Gopal luked at me with surprise and asked you also crying?

I sed yes after oll he is doing oll this for Muslims.

Gopal thout and then sed from today no more play of Hindu Muslim fite.

I sed yes after oll stoping fite we also must stop. When oll caching ears and swaring not to fite we also cach our ears.

Then we deside we will brake gun pistel bows arrows everything and thro in see.

And when I luk at Mohan the pore refooji boy for fust time I see small hapines in his eyes and I think it is like majik.

Next day father also sed Gandhiji done majik in Delhi and oll Hindus and Muslims and Sikhs caching their ears and swaring not to fite and Muslims getting their mosks and everything olrite in Delhi. So we are hapy to here you broke your fast and also go to tomb of Muslim saint Khaja Qutbuddin at time of Urs.

I and Gopal yesterday had agree to brake gun and pistel

atsetra but now when I see gun oll shiny and brite I don't like braking it and throing in see. Also I think suppose Gopal not brake his pistel why not I also keep gun. I not using it after oll only keeping it for sum rite moment.

Gopal aksi thout same suppose Annu not brake gun why I loos my pistel.

After you broke fast we felt beter. Sumhow when we herd you sick and week, hart was trubled like father or mother be sick. Not only I and Gopal but oll people. Now I know why oll call you Bapu.

Then one morning we hear bad news sumone throo bomb on you. Thank Gaud you were olrite and man who throo bomb arrested.

I say to Gopal—Gopal this is very bad. Bad people want kill Gandhiji. Gopal says yes we must gard Gandhiji life.

I sed how.

He sed we will go to Delhi and stand lik soljers to gard Gandhijis house.

I sed suppose sum bad people come and what you can do without gun or sord...

He spoke in hury why I have pistel and bows and arros. Then he bekum quait at once like he spoke by mistaik.

I also spoke in jury without thinking. What is pistel. I will gard with my gun.

Gopal luked at me and sed were you got gun from.

I also speek like that, from were you got pistel and arros.

He sed angrily you Musllims are like that no one can beleev you. You promised to brake gun.

Why I shud remane quait. I also speek angrily you Hindus tell lies. You promised to brake pistel.

Go I don't want play with you he sed.

We are not dyeing to play with you. I sed and came home and tuk out gun cleaned it and put oil in its mashinry. I must prepare for fite with Hindu Sena.

In thair hous Gopal and his brother also sit and prepare thair pistel and arros and bow.

Next time I see Mohan the pore refooji boy I see sem old feer in his eyes.

Days passed. One evning we are playing on see beech in frunt of our house when father comes rushing from offis and says Gandhiji ded, killed by some mad man.

Fust no one beleev but radio also say Gandhiji ded so have to beleev. Then I though see no one gard him proper. How man with pistel go nere him. I wish I and Gopal not wuareld and gone to gard Gandhiji at Delhi

That nite no one eat oll sitting near radio. We hed. Pandit Jawaharlal Nehru he is so grate man but weeping like childs. Speeking and weeping oll time. So I also cry with with teers. Every one cry. Even teers in eyes of father.

I kud not sleep proper. I saw in bad dreems bad man coming to kill you and I crying shouting save Gandhiji his life in danjer but no one listen. Most dreem I saw bad man shuting you with my gun. And I thout that is why you bekum angry with me and go away to haven.

It was hurtal next day and eskool klosed. But our hart not in play. On boundry wol I see Mohan and he crying. Seeing him I also cry agen. Gopal comes he also crying.

Gopal Bapuji is gone.

I sed yes grandmother says Allah has kalled him to haven.

Then Gopal says I saw in dream.

My hart fills with feer so I say. You saw in dream that sum one killing with my gun.

No no Gopal says crying. I see in dreem sum one killing Bapu with my pistel…

I tell him about my dreem. Gopal says bapu angry with us both so gon away to haven, Then all of us cru and don't know what to do.

p.s.

February 13

I rote this letar many days before but not put in post
thinking I forgotten to rite sumthing important. Now I rite
it.

Yesterday your ashes were put in meny rivers and sees.
On chopati we see with our own eyes. Very meny people in
proseshun also meny Muslims oll crying with teers.

You will be glad to heer our gorement cach many bad
people who want kill you and make Hindus Muslims fite.
And in Pakistan, Hindustan oll Hindus Musllims caching
thair eers and swaring never fite again. Now you axkuse them
and come back.

Yesterday evning after oll people go away I vent to see
beech and brake my guan and thro it in wotar. There I also see
Gopals pistel and arros and bow lying broken in wotar.

So now oll of us myself Gopal Bundoo Zenab Sakina
Seeta oll cach our eers and sware we will never fite agen. Please
axkuse us and kum back.

You will kum back, wont you, Bapu?

In many ways this 'letar' is baffling. Abbas could as well have
made an adult write the same epistle because correct spellings
were not an Indian strength in any case. The poignancy of the
outpourings of a child cannot be discounted, and they remain
with us for a long time. Abbas was, even at the time of publication
of this letter, a big name in English writing, as journalist and
novelist. He was compared to Voltaire and 'an Indian subjective
version of John Gunther' on the book jacket. To Indians, Abbas
is known as the scriptwriter of cinema classis like *Awara* and
Shri 420, writer of 'The Last Page' column which ran in *Blitz*
magazine from 1941 to 1986. He died in 1987. The last page
of the iconoclastic leftist weekly (till it changed tack in its dying

phase) had more attractions than the Abbas column. This is not to suggest that his column survived on reflected glory. Alongside the column was always a pin-up, with rhymed couplets like this one: 'Nalini makes a winsome bather/But will someone blow off the lather?'

It was left to Abbas to blow the lather off the country's body politic and tell us some truths over the forty years that he wrote. The Indian-English letter is yet another indication of how he brought in a novelist's sensibilities to journalism.

7

GLOSSARIES AND HOW-TO'S
Rapidex, Hobson-Jobson, Hanklyn-Janklyn

Denting: Not the infliction of dents but their removal
and the restoration of the surface
—Entry in *Hanklyn-Janklyn*

Dictionaries and glossaries are doorways to instant linguistic expertise. Each new word appropriated into one's repertoire and then thrown at an unsuspecting listener during a casual conversation—or better still at a presentation—is a passport to instant stardom. New words can often serve as showpieces of calibre and advancement. A list of easy-to-grab, easy-to-mouth words is thus an irresistible attraction. To mug up such words and then mouth them is a temptation difficult to resist. The dictionary and the glossary are not just proponents of new knowledge, they are also viable commercial propositions. Many see it as a passport to a new world, as we shall see in this chapter.

In G. V. Desani's comic classic *All About H. Hatterr,* the eponymous protagonist flees the Scottish Christian society which adopted him since, among other reasons, he found the 'constant childhood preoccupation with the whereabouts of my mother unbearable'. The two things he took with him while he escaped are interesting:

> And one warm Indian autumn night, I bolted as planned having pinched for voluntary study, an English dictionary, the Rev. Head's own authored *Latin Self-Taught* and *French Self-Taught,* the Missionary Society's school stereoscope complete with my slides (my second love after my mother) and sufficient Missionary funds lifted from the Head's pocket to see me through life...

Bolting with a dictionary is even now seen as an assurance of advancement.

The dictionary was the first effort to codify the language and to rein it in. It was also part of the effort to label speakers of the standard form of the language as the elite class. The rest had to be kept out or taught some proper lessons. Though dictionaries help keep the language unsullied and serve as a valve or filter of new words, they are also a barrier to the spread of any language. Dictionaries codify but have not been known to be catalysts to linguistic osmosis.

One of the primary factors that fuelled the growth or interest in Indian-English in the vast Indian hinterland is the dictionaries and the how-to-learn-English books. If a letter-writer swears by Rapidex, he is not referring to a muscle relaxant that he pops in every time he has spasms about what to write in the next letter. Rapidex is among the top brands in India, even if one stacks it up with the big adspend consumer brands. Its mission: to teach Indians how to speak English. By a conservative estimate, it would have sold close to ten million copies in the thirty years since it was first published as a humble venture from a hole in the wall in the crowded Chawri Bazaar of Old Delhi.

'My father thought up this idea when he was a small bookseller. He wrote some of it himself and finally it took this shape,' said his engineer son Rohit Gupta, who tends to be extremely secretive and handles marketing for Pustak Mahal, the publishing house which his father set up after the incredible success of Rapidex. The book has now been translated into nineteen languages and Gupta, pointing to a sheaf of papers on his table, said, 'This is the contract for our nineteenth language edition. English-Sinhala.'

The *Rapidex English Speaking Course,* as the book is called, offers to teach spoken English in sixty days. It is a lesson-a-day format, and by the time the reader reaches the sixtieth day he would be expected to have memorized most English usage.

The incredible success of Rapidex, with its sales surpassing that of any original Indian title, is not due to any marketing savvy or because Gupta decoded and demystified the English language. All that the senior Gupta did was step into a vacuum. By the 1970s, millions of Indians had realized the importance of English in personal advancement. Few English-speaking and English-writing Indians remained out of work. Even illiterate but English-speaking people got jobs. Jobs were created to accommodate an English-speaking person in the front offices of many companies.

The urge and the need to know English already existed. Gupta's timing was the factor. In the mid-1970s, English was just coming into its own in the country after shaking off the bias against it many years after the British left. It wasn't easy those days to publicly announce love for English, though English-medium schools (read missionary schools) had already become popular and had succeeded in creating an aura about English.

The new generation was already being divided into the English-knowing elite and the riff-raff. The large numbers of youngsters in the Hindi heartland and in the south, especially those who did not have the benefit of English education, also wanted to be there. Rapidex held out the promise of delivering the same goods as English-medium schools. For millions in the last thirty years, it was just what they were looking for.

From 1976, when it was first published, Rapidex has had the same kitschy cover. The emphasis was not just on English: the fact that it could be learnt in a hurry—two months—that seemed to be key. The cover title is interestingly written in Hindi and not in English, even though spoken English is the holy grail which is here on offer. Not a single English word graces the front or back cover. 'Rapidex' is not written with classic curlicues but with speed lines cut across its face, suggesting motion. The subliminal suggestion was of course that it was the highway to prosperity via the language of English and that too at 'super-fast' speed. The typography suggesting speed in Rapidex has been recreated in a pain balm called Fast Relief, which is endorsed by Amitabh Bachchan. The faster the relief from being a Hindi-speaking villager, the better. It has all got to do with breaking the shackles of being bracketed in a world of no-hopers.

Rohit did not seem to think that there is any specific formula that helped in making Rapidex the all-time Indian bestseller.

'English is a world language. If I know English, I can survive anywhere. I can survive in South India also. When everything is governed by English, what do you do?' Rohit said, underlying the fast-held belief that English opens the door to new worlds. What is surprising is how this has become a conviction throughout the Hindi-speaking heartland of India, which is also the repository of deplorable poverty, with large numbers of non-aspirational poor, and people whose utter lack of civic sense and cleanliness have reduced some of India's most popular cities like Jaipur and Agra into stinking dumps where cows, dogs and groups of poor people scavenge for the next meal.

All this makes the Rapidex success curiouser. A whole lot of me-too imitations have hit the market since then, but nothing seems able to nibble away the brand equity of Rapidex. The price is just ₹110, though it would have sold as well for ₹200. But the intention here, as Rohit admitted, is to make it unattractive for plagiarizing. 'What is the profile of your buyer?' I asked him. 'It could be a graduate from a small town, it could be anyone who aspires for a job.' By way of explaining the aspirational nature of the Indians he caters to, Rohit asks, 'Who doesn't want to sit in an airplane? That desire is automatically there.'

Rapidex is a hurried run through everyday cliched conversational English and offers English equivalents for Indian usages on every conceivable occasion. A Rapidex user looking for romantic comeuppance is likely to turn to the section on love letters on page 417, which comes after the sections Letters of Condolence and Letters of Thanks, and ponder over sixteen possible lines which include opening sentences and sign-offs. The introduction to the chapter written in Hindi informs readers, with rustic naivete, that there are two types of love letters, one exchanged between the husband and wife and the other between lovers. The basic nature of the tutorial offered in the book could be another reason for its success.

The first part consists of four sentences on how to begin a love letter in English:

1. Your loving letter this morning has come like a ray of sun-shine
2. Your sweet letter has enveloped me in the sweet fragrance of our love

3.   Your letter has flooded me with sheer happiness
4.   Your affectionate letter has dispelled the depression that
     surrounded me earlier

After listing sixteen possible sentences that could hopefully send the romantic impulses in the receiver of the letter ratcheting up, Rapidex, moving with super speed towards the end of its crash course, gives a sample letter which is a collection or putting together of the sixteen lines laid out in the beginning of the chapter. Just in case.

> Dearest…
> Your sweet letter has enveloped me in the sweet fragrance of our love. Everything is fine here except that I miss you so badly. Write back soon as your letters provide me a great emotional support, You are the greatest thing that happened to my life…

Well, quite basic and well within the limits of cliched writing apart from a brief departure into metaphorical 'sweet fragrance of our love'.

But before the Hindi-speaking Romeo of an urban mohalla or a mofussil Dev Anand trying to reach out to the English-speaking girl who is the receptionist at an office he frequents reaches page 417 he is taken through a wide gamut of usages and opening lines, most of which are a collection of cliches and set pieces. But then innovative language is not possible in a basic how-to book of this sort.

Rapidex comes with a free cassette which the preface promises will help the reader gather confidence in speaking English with the right pronunciation. But before he reaches that stage he would have glanced at what to say where and why. The conversational section starts at page 175. Situations like asking questions to a shopkeeper are written in Hindi on the left side and explained in English on the right side. The English usages are then written out in Hindi or Devnagari script for good measure. It is not easy because 'Please' is often written or pronounced in Hindi as 'Pleej'.

No one has come out in open praise of Rapidex for increasing their level of confidence or social interaction. But each purchase is a renewal of confidence. Nor has Rapidex so far published the pictures of successful candidates for India's big civil services exams, who depended on the glossary. The irony is that the bestselling book has a terribly down-market image and people in cities especially wouldn't be seen dead with it. I placed a copy of Rapidex on my office desk for a day and soon enough people who passed by my desk were ribbing me. A colleague picked up the book, held it up, burst into laughter and announced: 'Binoo's great English secret.' Five people took up the book from my desk, held it up, examined it and passed dismissive comments. Another colleague who worked with former cricket captain and national hero Kapil Dev then joined us and gave us a real, embarrassing anecdote about Kapil Dev's English. But then Kapil Dev is not embarrassed, nor are millions of others like him, denied an English-medium education but always knocking at the doors of the elite club of English speakers.

The only time Rapidex went on a promotional spree was when it hired Kapil Dev to endorse the product. Kapil Dev was the right icon for Rapidex, for he was a non-English speaking achiever. In other words, non-English speakers are not marketed as achievers. Anyone who achieves something is bound to know English. That is the common but misguided perception. When Kapil Dev held high the 1983 World Cup trophy in the balcony of Lord's, it was not just a sporting victory. With the wisdom of hindsight we can now say that it put India on the road to supreme confidence as a nation, and gave people faith in themselves and their country. Thanks to television the 1983 World Cup allowed people to partake of the victory, quite unlike the Olympic hockey victories. Participatory triumphalism is better than remote-sensed victory celebrations.

The immediate benefit was visible in the way cricket became a symbol of national identity with which the country would hit back at Empire. A nation of many languages had found a weapon of unified self-expression. Any sport is a great leveller, but to India cricket was a great unifier. Cricket became the language not just of commerce and sport but of back-slapping jingoism. Everyone understood the language of cricket. The scores, the names of players, the over rates, the number of boundaries, the comparative run rate—all this did not require a language of communication. Indians love numbers and cricket threw up its share of numbers and statistics that Indians on the teeming streets could crunch and munch along with their bhelpuris and aloo tikkis. By that time the radio had made way for television, every Indian embraced the small screen just as he had the big screen. The difference was that the big screen sold dreams and an escape route. The small screen brought euphoric reality. It was also to bring its share of disappointments and moments of eternal self-flagellation. It happened when Pakistan's Javed Miandad lofted a six off the last ball in a tournament in India. Such moments made us wonder whether Indians at all had the killer instinct.

In the midst of that stood Kapil Dev with the World Cup on the balcony of Lord's. It was an image that would emboss itself on the minds of millions of Indians. The toothy grin that morphed a rustic innocence with high achievement went straight to the heart of the big unknown, underachieving India. That image, that victory was an incendiary trigger that would light up an Indian's mind in times of national defeats and sorrows, which were many.

It was that underachieving India that Rapidex catered to. It too needed a symbol. Kapil could have done with a rapid course in English which was faulty in the traditional sense but quite acceptable to the Hindi heartland. Yet, he needed the finishing that Rapidex promised. He was the right fit for Rapidex in a strange way, and even though Rohit was unwilling to acknowledge if the Kapil endorsement did boost its sales, the Indian's yearning to learn English was aligned with the yearning to achieve.

Around that time or a little later Kapil also endorsed the Palmolive shaving cream with a guttural and full-mouthed 'Palmolive *da jawab nahin*' (Palmolive has no answer), a Punjabi catchline that, like the other two images with which Kapil was associated, would go right to the heart of the real aspiring India. There was no answer nor equal to Kapil. He had already held aloft the cup of achievement. The Indian cup of joy was overflowing. Whether they bought Palmolive shaving cream is not known, but Rapidex sure kicked up a lather across Hindi-speaking India. They wanted to achieve, they wanted to be up there in the champagne-soaked balcony of universal glory, looking down at the cheering multitudes below.

Maybe Rapidex would have sold without Kapil as well, but the endorsement with him holding up a copy of the Hindi-English usage dictionary was bizarre as well as captivating. The endorsement was paradoxical in a way. Even that paradox worked. A sportsman (not a cerebral Anil Kumble-like cricketer) had become the icon for education and literacy. A non-English speaker was selling one of the biggest how-to-speak-English books, a man who is not even a graduate was endorsing a book for thousands of graduates. It was a call to higher education and higher achievement that held millions of Indians in an asphyxiating grasp.

The Rapidex copyrighted brand has been used in a wide range of books on how to weather the various storms in your life, how to use your PC with Microsoft Windows, 101 ways to prepare kababs, 2,000 titbits and *Satires to Make you Grin, Smirk and Laugh*. The Rapidex attempt at refining the multitudes of perceptively crass but literate Indians and in the process making a brand is an unacknowledged and unacclaimed success in Indian marketing. The Gupta family is not too keen to become grist to success stories for the media. It is not that they do not like success but that they, like most Indian businesses, underplay their achievements.

One reason that the Rapidex concept caught on was the day-to-day teaching that it was patterned after. Everything was compartmentalized. The third day, for instance, is devoted to learning exclamations. 'Marvellous', 'Well done', 'How sweet', 'How disgraceful' are explained in Hindi and then again written in Hindi or Devanagari script. The fourth day lessons are devoted to phrases. 'Just coming', 'As you please', 'Not a bit', 'Rest assured', 'Long time no see', and other such Indian favourites are also explained.

There could be problems, though. A person who imbibes these lessons is bound to get tied up in knots till he gets help from an English-speaking person or move in an English-supporting environment. Sentences like 'Rest assured if you mend your ways', 'Thank you for your letter which emits fragrance', if the user picks up point 10 from one chapter and point 4 from another.

The process of understanding India and Indian usages started quite early. It had to start with the British.

Sir Charles Napier wrote this note quoted in *Hobson-Jobson*:

1844, headquarters, Kurrachee 12th February. The Governor unfortunately does not understand Hindostanee, nor Persian, nor Mahratta nor any other eastern dialect. He therefore will feel particularly obliged to Collectors, sub-collectors and officers writing the proceedings of Courts-martial and all Staff Officers to indit'e their various papers in English, larded with as small portion of the to him unknown tongues as they conveniently can, instead of those he generally receives—namely Hindostanee larded with occasional words in English.

Hobson-Jobson, a glossary of Indian-English words, was compiled by Henry Yule in collaboration with A. C. Burnell. Compilations being a British speciality, it is no wonder that *Hobson-Jobson* turned out to be a classic which inspired yet another updated modern classic called *Hanklyn-Janklyn*, both of which traced the etymology of Indian words with baffling precision, a sense of history and impish humour.

The post-independence *Hanklyn-Janklyn* compiled by New Delhi-based recluse the late Nigel Hankin is part two of *Hobson-Jobson* and is a 'stranger's rumble-tumble guide to some words, customs and quiddities Indian and Indo-British'. The complexity of the Indian encounter with the West was sought to be simplified by these two glossaries. In the process, they have done a lot for our etymological understanding and also hold out a clue as to how Indian words get sucked in by English and vice-versa. Hankin's detailing is incredible, as is his understanding of Indian idioms and social practices. All of this of course tinged with that understated humour. His entry for The Ear Cleaner is one such impish effort:

An urban itinerant professional gentleman identified by his small red puggri into which are tucked his instruments;

tweezers, probes and buds of cotton wool on wooden splints.
He will attend his clients anywhere on the roadside in the
bazaar, in the shade of a park tree or at places of work or
homes: peering and probing into ears for wax and producing
for inspection the evidence of his skills. Bat as with the
providers of other personal services in the bazaar, such as the
bihisti and this maleesh wala, public demand is no longer
what it was and the trade of the kan mailiyan/kan bhedi—the
ear cleaner—seems to be a dying one.

And this one for 'heating foods', a typical Indian-English
usage which looks quite innocent at first go—but beneath lie
layers of Indianized meanings and mythology.

Euphemism for foods thought to enhance sexual strength and
passion (heating) in the human body, chiefly animal proteins
and eggs. The reverse is achieved by cooling foods, mostly
vegetable, but not entirely almonds (badam) for example, are
thought to be particularly invigorating. The theory comes
from ayurveda. The Chinese, Malays, and some other Asian
peoples, similarly categorise their food and drink. Those who
wish to lead a godly and contemplative life are recommended
to avoid heating foods; in general they are considered ill-
advised for women and firmly to be avoided by widows.

Not satisfied by these notings on the history of just one type of
food classification, Hankin goes even further into mythology:

A Vedic classification, still accepted by some, divided food
into sattvik, rajasik and tamasik. Sattvik (satv: pertaining to
purity, righteousness and virtue) foods are simple natural and
vegetarian: such as dairy products and honey, gur, vegetables—
excluding garlic and onions and some will aver, exotics like
the chilli and tomato, fruit and cereals. Rajasik (of the good

things in life, pertaining to kingship) items are high protein: fish, eggs meat and wines. Tamasik foods (tamas: darkness and ignorance) are forbidden to all caste Hindus: beef, village pork (but wild boar is sometimes included in the rajasik category, particularly by Rajputs) fish without scales (eg eels) and spirits. In these days some consider any convenience food out of a tin or packet to be tamasik. See also panchama.

Explaining India and its English usages to a large audience has never been taken up as meticulously and arduously as Hankin and Yule-Burnell have done. The British or the Western fascination for things Indian, more so the language, is symbolized in these two glossaries.

Hankin has this adulatory entry for *Hobson-Jobson*.

Title of a famous glossary by Henry Yule of Anglo-Indian words and phrases, unique in style, erudition and above all, readability.

... The glossary was reviewed in April 1888 for his paper by a twenty-one year old reporter of the daily *Civil and Military Gazette* of Lahore (total editorial staff two) one Rudyard Kipling: '...unless we are much mistaken, it will take its place amongst the standard works on the east, and will pass, gathering bulk as it goes, from decade to decade.

Yule and Burnell set out to search out words, mostly administrative, which are in 'quotidian use as to form part of the common Anglo-Indian stock'. It was a job that lasted many years and was not completed before the death of Burnell of the Madras Civil Service, who was mostly based in South India, while Yule was based in Palermo. The book originated out of casual letters among the two. Both of them had compiled such usages and after meeting just once and after exchange of letters decided to combine their efforts. It was bound to be a classic combine.

The work they put in can be seen from how they traced the origins of some Indian words which have become commonplace in English. The common word tank, they traced back to the Spanish *stagnum* and the old French *estang* and lowland Scotch *stank* and Portuguese *tanque*.

The name *Hobson-Jobson* is also a resonance of the Indian habit of rhyming double words or echo words mostly using English and Hindi words in a bilingual coupling that has grown so popular in Indian usage that it has found its way into journalism and literature as well. The hyphenated usage of rhyming words could possibly have started in Bengal, where this practice is more prevalent than in the Hindi heartland.

So I wasn't surprised to see this Rediff.com report from Kolkata which went online without being edited, a victim of the cut-and-paste journalism of the Internet age, scoffing at the old-school way of scrutinizing usages and trying to improve them. The Rediff.com reporter from Kolkata was a typical practitioner, and he sent this rocket on 29 April 2005, which was proudly displayed on the home page of the widely read news website. 'Greg Chappel seems a front runner for the job of Indian coach but cricket officials shilly-shallying over the selection could prove costly as Sri Lanka too is eyeing the Australian great.'

Shilly-shallying is of course an Indianized version of dilly-dallying. It could actually be just a Bengali innovation since shilly-shallying can usually be heard only in spoken language (though Rushdie uses it in *Midnight's Children).* Till this website reporter took it upon himself to adopt a musical echo in the opening lines of his dispatch.

Soon enough the reporter, however, seems to have realized that he is taking a risk. In the next paragraph, he again comes to the same phrase but decides to use the original accepted English word rather than go for his own creation. 'Bangladesh took advantage of India's dilly-dallying and offered Whatmore an extension.'

Better writers too have put such echo words to good use, the most well-known among them being Salman Rushdie himself, who took an immortal ride through the nooks and crannies of Indian-English in *Midnight's Children*. He did not miss the echo words either. The protagonist-narrator is admonished for his 'writery-shitery' life.

A clincher about Indian-English users is that they do not dilly-dally when it comes to choosing words, creating, modifying and letting them loose upon the world. It is not strange that both the British compilers of Indian words chose what Hankin calls 'jingle or echo' words as titles for their great glossaries. Hankin gives an elaborate reason for the choice of title:

Why Hanklyn-Janklin? The words have no meaning of course, but I would like to think of them not as a plagiarism but as a resonant tribute to the much more accomplished commentator than I of 1886, Henry Yule, and his work on roughly the same subject, Hobson-Jobson. The commercial reason advanced by Colonel Yule for his choice has not escaped my notice: in a bookshop, a volume with a main title of a glossary of something is likely to be perceived as a textbook or, at least not for the general reader. It also happens that jingle or echo words are quite common in Indian family speech; one may give a party-warty, where one may drink a whisky-pisky or a cup of chai-wai. If bored, one may move ass-pass (nearby) and read a kitab-witab.

Hankin was quite definite about using echo words and he didn't have to shilly-shally about the title.

Among the many words that Hankin digs out as Indian contribution to English is denting, the popular national term for repair work of car bodies. 'An Indian-English term in connection with the body work of vehicles, not the infliction of dents but their removal and the restoration of the surface.' As Hankin points out, denting is used in the opposite sense of what it actually means. It does not mean that the repairman, the ustaad of the Hindi heartland, is going to dent the car but instead smoothen out the dents. '*Gaadi* denting *karenge* (I will do denting)', the roadside mechanic assures you.

The famous Delhi Belly, the expression which carried the name of the Indian capital to other parts of the world, is explained thus: 'A stomach disorder sometimes afflicting newcomers to the capital: akin to Gippy tummy of Egypt; the Montezuma's Revenge of Mexico, the Turkey Trots of Istanbul and the Kathmandu Quickstep of Nepal. As a pleasantry, Delhi Belly can be the increase of girth, of rotundity, often observed on a diplomat after a year of the capital's social whirl.'

When I met Hankin after a two-month search-and-wait, he looked just the way I remembered him from my two previous meetings almost a decade back. Six-foot-two at least, the eighty-six-year-old Brit who was a permanent resident of India ('This is home') was waiting for me in the bookshop which the publisher of *Hanklyn* ran in Khan Market. He was a recluse and it was only a register kept in the Mughal Gate of the British High Commission in Delhi that was his communication link to the outside world. But I had requested his publisher to alert me on his once-in-three-weeks arrival at the shop. He had the stride of a lumbering giraffe surveying its far-flung terrain. When he raised his head, his eyes were darting restlessly behind his thick-rimmed spectacles. We sat at a nearby coffee shop, the space too cramped for his long legs that had trodden the gullies of Delhi over the last half-century as it reshaped itself after every national trauma. His roads were where princes, conquerors and pillagers plotted and carried out their big moves. The past was Hankin's terrain. That was where his soul was most comfortable. That was where his stories stemmed from. That was why he lived in a time-warp, uncaring of the present, contemptuous of the future and constantly refusing to sell out.

'I knew every street in Delhi and its history. But I don't care for the new parts of the city that spreads outwards.' It was by taking others around the nooks and crannies of Delhi's history that Hankin earned a living. His clients were mostly based in Delhi. Or the choosy traveller who needed to shoot questions at the guide as he surveyed the marbled walls of Diwan-i-Khas in the Red Fort.

Every evening Hankin walked to the Mughal Gate of the embassy in the swanky diplomatic enclave of Delhi and opened his register to see if there were any clients who had asked for him. 'I sign it and write confirmed,' he said with a swish of his hands. He would meet the tourists at the embassy gate at the date written on the register and take them for walks in areas agreed upon. The eye for detail which Hankin displayed in his glossary was in evidence as one walked with him to learn the history of Delhi, which has the most historical monuments, not counting Rome. Hankin was Delhi's unparalleled oral historian. On a walk with him a decade back, I remember him standing near a rock in Old Delhi, looking at the grand sweep of Delhi in front and recreating the mutiny of 1857 as if he was history's immortal chronicler. What he knew about Delhi few historians know. I suggested that he should write it all down. He was not opposed to the idea; at eighty-six, he wouldn't mind another beginning.

I asked him how he managed to dig out the etymology

of Indian words and usages with such precision and detail. 'Newspapers and books here and there.' He seemed to suggest that it was done with effortless ease, as if it was part of his calling. He started on the effort after he got requests off and on from British residents in Delhi and the embassy on the meaning of various Hindi usages that found their way into everyday conversational English. Once a newly arrived doctor in the British embassy called Sidney Hamilton gave him a list of 'some twenty Indian words' he had read in local English newspapers which had foxed him. Out of that list was born *Hanklyn-Janklyn*.

After we finished the coffee and sandwiches, Hankin took the same lumbering strides back to the nearby shop of his publisher to get his royalty statement, which was due to him for a long time. He shrugged his shoulders as if to say it was all part of the baggage of being a writer in India. He had already finished the next set of words to update the glossary.

Hankin passed away in Delhi in 2009, unsung and forgotten, and maybe in penury. Only one newspaper in Delhi took note of his passing.

8

HATTER, TROTTER AND OTHER WRITTEN MATTER

'I am hoping all is well with health and wealth. I am
fine at my end. Hoping your end is fine too'
—Gopal's letter to his brother in
The Inscrutable Americans

Police officer S. Saleem, author of *Mudly*, though inspired
by Nehru, did not just satisfy himself writing a paean and
hoping that posterity would beckon him for a pat on the back.
He hoped that his novel would be picked up by a film producer
and that his crime thriller would revive the dying art of writing
Indian novels in English. Ambition was, of course, a plus point
with the intelligence officer. But how a crime thriller could have
helped the country rid itself of financial ills, as his introduction
states, is a matter of conjecture. Unless he was thinking of
earning enough foreign exchange from his book to even out
the country's trade deficit. It must have been his Oxford degree

which gave Saleem the idea of prodding awake the slumbering giant of Indian fiction writing and sending it off to conquer new worlds. And, in the process, if it helps the country move towards a surplus budget, then of course it would be an added benefit!

Saleem's introduction reflects his concern about the state of Indo-Anglian writing and the absence of bestsellers and goes on to offer his novel as the panacea. Not surprisingly, Saleem expresses the hope that *Mudly* will be a bestseller. Saleem believed that bestsellers are a matter of divine intervention rather than any Gamma Beta Phi qualities in the writer.

> Paucity of novels, written in India in English is well known. I do not know of any that has proved a best seller in the sense the term is used in Europe and America. If this one proves a best seller, it would encourage writers generally. For a best seller it is not necessary to have any extraordinary merit. The miracle just happens, and leave people wondering. The book has been written with an eye on the screen in the hope it may catch the eye of an enterprising Producer, gifted with imagination. It is a simple story, simply told. The theme is as old as the hills—A marriage market scene at the Simla fair, a China Town scene at Calcutta, and life as lived in different hotels, would undoubtedly make a first class Movie attraction. The author has done his part and it is for others now to join force. S.S

Saleem's vaulting ambition of writing a bestseller and in the process injecting a dose of life-giving elixir to the moribund art of novel writing in English may have been out of place considering that Indo-Anglian novels were being talked about. By that time a host of Gandhian and Nehruvian novels in English by writers like R. K. Narayan, Raja Rao and Mulk Raj Anand had served notice of their intention and literary might. Anand had dominated the two previous decades, and it is a surprise that an Oxford-educated officer did not seem to have noticed and thus did not bother to pay tribute to these big names. Saleem hadn't yet connected with mainstream writing, one should guess. Was he doomed to remain on the fringes, with Indian-English for company? But the attempt was nevertheless made and with the wisdom of hindsight we can say that Saleem can be proud of writing the thriller *Mudly* considering the slew of big works that followed immediately after independence and Partition!

To write a novel in English, just like speaking well in English or writing the classified insert in English or resorting to English for the hoarding announcing the latest in baldness cure, is all part of the overwhelming longing among Indians to be part of a global phenomenon or the longing to be tagged along with 'big peoples who talk always English, no?' Like Saleem, who ended up with an Indian-English novel which was duly forgotten and fated to gather dust in unsearched library racks, many others who could have written in Indian languages opted for English, unable to see the language as a minefield.

The successful writers, the original Englishwallahs, by the privileges of birth and resultant entry into the elitist world where English ruled, had no such handicap. They knew how to mould the language to project the Indian experience for a global audience. Indian-English was very much part of the Indian experience, and here we look at those who used the higher forms of English to caricature it and in the process produced novels that have become benchmarks.

Saleem's novel is not a benchmark in the literary history of English writing in India, but it definitely is a benchmark Indian-English work, as the few lines quoted here will show. The theme of a police officer in search of a criminal is a fit subject for a novel written for the movies. We enter the novel here as the officer is in close contact with the pretty lady whom he chanced upon in the Savoy Hotel in 'Massourie'. This scene happens at the Savoy Hotel. The other chapters too are set in hotels across the world.

> I took her hand and pressed it and said 'I would do anything for you. Even forgive that Letter J'. 'Oh! His name is Jogu, a fearful man but let us not talk of him tonight,' she said. As I sat at the table with her, I could not conceal from myself that meeting her had given me a joy of a kind I had never felt before…her dream, her jewels, her poise, everything gave the impression that she was out to conquer. And it was to conquer me that she was out. I could not feel bucked and flattered.

With this plot and Indian-English phraseology and syntax we are convinced that it was to conquer the world of Indian novels that Saleem was out!

The police officer and the lady, Pretty, continue their meetings.

> Dinner that evening tasted far better than other evenings and it was for the first time since arrival, I found myself really enjoying.
>
> At the end of every course we got up and danced. Rizvi my friend who belong to the same service as myself came in later into the Dining hall to find me engaged with a young lady to his great surprise.

Mudly is not possessive about the lady and lets Rizvi too dance with Pretty, who expresses admiration for Rizvi's dancing.

> 'Your friend is a good dancer', Pretty said and added. You are a bit on the heavy side.'
>
> 'But if I continue dancing like this I would soon be on the lighter side,' I said.

'If I have your schooling, I would soon polish you up, as a horse is polished in the morning,' she replied.

'I am very fond of horses you know, but would not care to be rubbed like that,' I said.

'Nice soft loving hands would rub you but you would not understand that till you are married,' she said.

'Perhaps I am married,' I said. 'I wish you were,' she said and added 'then the inner voice in me would stop me from worrying about you.'

The sexually charged dinner meeting which threatened to get a bit horsey was cut short by the revelation that Mudly was a married man. Otherwise, the duo would have polished each other up, leaving the curvy and rippling biceps of English shining with new meaning. If Saleem hadn't cut short that dinner meeting in what now reads like a hilarious adolescent narration, his sexual encounter would have been something like this, I imagine.

'Like Cherry Blossom?'

'Nice polish. I can polish you up in one day. If only you allow me some clock time.'

'If you like, I like. I apply. You reply ok Pretty?'

'I use my soft hands. Even on the belly which is on the heavier side.'

'You use brush on the underbelly.'

'Soft hands of mine are better on unmarried people. Others will be caught with their pants down.'

'Brush me pleej. Polish me. Give me digital polish with your digits…' I took her hand and pressed it again for the second time during the dinner. It sent tinglings through my nerve endings and rang the bells for a new matter of my heart in my life.

Saleem did not set out to write a comic classic, but the language sends a tingle up and down the spine of puritans. Saleem set out to write in English with a view to impressing Nehru and others in the higher echelons of society. For him, as for many others, it was a vehicle for reaching out.

Many others did set out to write comic classics in English and achieved great success. G. V. Desani, who wrote the earliest Indian comic classic *All About H. Hatterr* (first published as *All About Mr Hatterr),* first gave English readers abroad a taste of Indian-English and the rare Indian art of satire. It was welcomed heartily and has survived all these years. To me, reading it more than fifty years later, it seemed a bit drab, and I didn't have to stifle any laughs building up in my innards. That I've-been-here-before feeling could be because many Indo-Anglian writers had, since Desani, played around with Indian-English usage with the confidence that comes from the mastery of English and its literary lineage. Desani, the inventor of a rare and difficult genre, paved the way for other such attempts, many of them finding a place in the sub-category of Indian novels in English poking fun at *dehati* people's nonsense-speaking habits and phoren-going Indians speaking English in New Yark (with many words not in Oxford dictionary, please note)!

Even today Desani's portrayal of the Indian who sought wisdom from the seven sages and his Bengali sidekick resonates with humorous situations and some set pieces. It is a caricature of the country through the medium of Indian-English. The literary world had a hearty laugh for many years. *Hatterr* has left a mark both for the comical nature of its plot and the Indian-English that underlies the narrative. It was the English of the non-Brit, of course. It has won admirers and critical acclaim all the way—from 1948, when it was first published by Aldor, reprinted two months later and reissued two years later by Saturn Press. Such initial hullabaloo was rarely created by an Indian author in the literary establishment in London. *Hatterr* is written in the mould of the search-for-truth narrative and has its moments. For the Western user of propah English, Desani's use of language was revelation and confirmation of what they always suspected: the polluting impact of Empire. The timing was just right

In the introduction to the 1972 edition of *Hatterr*, Antony Burgess points out how the critic F. W. Bateson made the distinction between the native English writer and the meteque— 'the writer with a non-English lingusitic, racial or political background who being on the fringe of a language and the culture that begot it, lacks respect for the finer rules of English idiom and grammar'. Burgess argues like many other critics after him that the pejorative meteques have done more for English in the twentieth century than any of the pure-blooded men of letters who stick to the finer rules.

Desani can be said to have scored a bull's eye with the Indian-English that the eponymous hero speaks. The constant breaching of the finer rules of grammar by any speaker is often the subject of mirth and Desani attains that effortlessly. Crassness, like ignorance, can easily be scoffed at. The slapstick situations in the novel, like when Hatterr is forced or lured into a circus where the prime attraction is the lion eating food laid out on his own sprawled body, are hilarious, all the more considering Hatterr's innocence about English and his grandiloquent summoning of phrases like 'cerebro-meningitis shiver'.

For sheer situational comedy, it is difficult to find something parallel to this in Indian writing:

> Midst the hot drumming [in the show] the steak was placed
> on my chest.

... then he approached. A cerebro-meningitis shiver shot through my spinal-cord as he [the lion] came nearer!

He made contact and commenced to crunch.

While he continued, I felt as if a mysterious supernatural thing was massaging me all over: first like the crawl of cheesmites on the derm, next the technique of pinching and kneading the skin, and I felt hellishly ticklish!

But the animal's bent head, it seemed magnified to about a thousand times an average zoo lion's made the very powerful urge to scratch and relieve instantly null and void.

Under the weight of the steak of meat, and the stress of a dam lion bending over, I gave up any illusion of ever rising again and of being resurrected to the living.

I more or less renounced the ghost and thought in the Julius Caesar vein...

Much of the rib-tickling effect in *Hatterr* is obtained by the splendid caricaturing of Hindu sadhus, or godmen, which has been a staple ingredient in Indian comedy, particularly cinema. Desani had everything that would serve up India to the lion of the English establishment. It tickled the Indians' fancy too. 'He speak, just like Indian speaking only, no...'

Hatterr could well have shown the way to the use of Indian-English as a comic device. It could also have given later authors the idea of garnering English words, giving them various twists and turns, inflecting a bit of Hindi, punning on them, trying out audacious turns of phrases, creating crass English usages—all of which go a long way in 'capturing the Indian experience'. This is the duty assigned to all Indian, non-resident Indian, formerly Indian, migrant Indian, Indian-born-but-fled, born-phoren-but grandfather-from-eastern-UP, and chutney-Indian writers of fiction. By appropriating non-Indians (like Uganda-born Desani did) to embellish the Indian canon (a pardonable national habit, considering the paucity of domestic talent), the list of such writers has grown. But Indian writing also has a grittiness which comes out of its evolution from a long rich tradition.

Salman Rushdie, who could easily belong to one or two of the above-mentioned categories of writers, could very well have got his idea of inventive use of the language from *Hatterr*. 'I'm very fond of that book. I thought it was the only book that attempted a reshaping of English in a radical way,' Rushdie has said about *Hatterr*. At the very least, he must have summoned the courage to take all sorts of lingusitic and grammatical licence from Desani.

Either way, Rushdie's inventiveness, the way he merrily let himself go in his magic-realist novel *Midnight's Children,* is also the high point of Indian-English which was satirized or used with aplomb. Here was the fringe language, the language used by the aspirant class, the language of the underachiever, finding a place in a grand and incredible novel that was an allegory for India's birth and evolution. Indian usages in English were not just caricatured—for the first time, they established a certain credibility and thus gave the patois a raison d'etre it had never enjoyed before. It was the daring attempt to use the language that Indians actually spoke, instead of the imagined and air-brushed genre that Indian writers were forced to use. Thus we see what the critic Meenakshi Mukherjee called 'getting away with the use of mongrel street language of cities, daring to translate idioms and metaphor with an audacious literalness and perpetrating bilingual puns mediated by no apology, no footnote, no glossary…'

Midnight's Children was in a way the beatification—if not the canonization—of that specifically Indian wayward language. If Hatterr spoke the language sometimes apologetically, often self-consciously and thus offered himself up to be scoffed at,

Rushdie's characters used the language as a badge of honour, and not just for holding themselves up to ridicule by the British, those mainstreamers. Rushdie's sentences had meanings which Indians could relate to wholeheartedly and prise out the layers of meaning and social critiques that many of those words portrayed. Etymology was thus one of the engine rooms that drove the narrative. Rushdie used no UV filters while offering up the grand Indian story for the Western reader. The colours were real and stark, though sometimes overexposed with the dazzling light of his imagery.

Unlike Desani, Rushdie had in his quiver the weapon of the surreal and the coda of the fabulist to transform his characters from the ordinary to the sublime. He had the power of magic realism, by which he could sort out the complexity of Indian reality with some deft linguistic hybridity. The surreal Indian reality, not interpreted and analysed reality, was what was needed. Rushdie kneaded the language as if it were dough, then tossed it with one sweeping motion into the scalding heat of the oven of his imagination. The lingering taste of the linguistic inventions, the chutneyfication—and oh, the puns—still thrill us. Indian literature would never be the same again. When Saleem Sinai went to a 'real real putty joint which advertises lassi, fantabulous, faluda and Bhelpuri Bombay fashion', he was tagging along with him a splay-footed new language which was all this while struggling to be born. It sent ripples across the cloistered world of Indian writing. From then on, Indian characters in novels could speak their own tongue and did not have to bother if some Englishman found fault with them for always having pudding-shudding and talking altu-faltu things.

Rushdie had foreseen the splash that a later hero of his would make when in *Grimus* (1979), the hero Flapping Eagle, an American Indian, goes in search of his lost sister and ends up in a Mediterranean island. Rushdie was thus examining the problems of the immigrant, and with *Midnight's Children,* he moved towards resolution with a splashing thud. With Flashing Eagle, Rushdie grappled with the question:

> Stripped of his past, forsaking the language of his ancestor for the language of the archipelagos of the world, forsaking the ways of his ancestors for those of the place he drifted to, forsaking any hopes of ideals in the face of the changing and contradictory ideals he encountered, he lived doing what he was given to do, thinking of what he was instructed to think, being what it was most desirable to be…

That play with Indian-English might be Rushdie's way of showing his intimacy with India and reclaiming the country as his, even as Indians always claimed Rushdie as an Indian writer. 'I am an Indian guy,' he told an interviewer after the publication of *Shalimar the Clown,* pointing to the fount of his inspiration from where he hasn't stopped drinking, every thirsty slurp just an excuse for another take. That urge to pay his dues, so to say, to Indian-English can be seen in *Shalimar,* the stirring story of love and revenge set in Kashmir and the US. Here it is the Indian, mostly bureaucratic, fascination for hi-falutin English phraseology that Rushdie takes off on. A well-meaning Kashmiri doctor, faced with a large number of injured and maimed people delivers this explanatory speech in the presence of some injured people, instead of getting down to the task of saving some lives if possible.

> 'It is my onerous obligation before proceeding', the young doctor said, 'to offer our obsequious apologies and to seek from you an obligatory clarification. This is odious but indispensable current routine. Heartfelt apology is primarily offered for understaffing. Many pandit personnel have

decamped and policy does not permit replacement. Many ambulance drivers also are being accosted by security forces and are being extremely chastised and therefore no longer are reporting for duty. Apology is secondarily offered for shortages of supplies. Asthma medication is unavailable. Treatment for diabetics is unavailable. Oxygen tanks are unavailable. Owing to load shedding certain medicament are not refrigerated and condition of said medicaments is dubious. Replacement however are unavailable. Apology is additionally offered for failure of all X-ray machines, sterilization devices and such equipment as is designed to analyse blood.

Apology is further extended owing to supply of blood not tested for HIV. Ultimate apology is regarding presence of meningitis epidemic in this facility and for impossibility of quarantining same. Guidance at this time is sought from your good selves. Under circumstance as sorrowfully outlined above you will kindly and severally confirm or de-confirm you wish to be admitted to or de-admitted from this facility so that treatment is able to proceed or de-proceed. Have no doubt, ladies and gentlemen, that if you trust in us we will make our best effort.'

Needless to say, none of the five victims survived. Led by bureaucracy's gazette English, such long-winded words have found precious space in the Indian mindset. The love of complicated phrases, the fascination with the roundabout way of putting a thing across, the undying urge to send the reader to mark out a word in red (for later check and recheck—in *Oxford Advanced Learner's Dictionary*, you know) is a trait close to Indian hearts. In this love for the complicated word, this allegiance to the thesaurus, this triumphant holding up of the bizarre phrase, this Rushdie replica of Indian-English bears close resemblance to Indian bureaucratese.

A circular issued by the Delhi High Court Bar Association on 28 September 2005 is indication that the above-mentioned trait is gathering steam. This circular refers to unethical practices by judges who have their 'nears and dears' practising in the same court. How closely Rushdie reflected the real!

1. Members of the Executive Committee through personal interaction with and oral information from the Hon'ble members (howsoever subjective or unfounded in reality their perception may be) feel that there is a kind of deja vu especially because of some kind of special treatment allegedly being meted out to the kith, kin erstwhile associates and chamber mates etc, etc, of the Hon'ble judges and this kind of entente cordiale, if coming into play, should be opposed and nipped in the bud.

It was all about someone breaking the shackles of language, and Rushdie did it with a bang four decades after Desani's giggly but no less masterful way of blending languages. Desani had no large canvas in mind, his ambition did not soar like Rushdie's (though Hatterr sure goes through some stomach-chomping moments) and everything revolved around the use of language. Yet, neither of them were Indian in the real sense. Desani wasn't even born in India, though he came to India to reclaim his identity and spent time learning yoga and undergoing mystical experiences.

Desani's inventiveness stretched to technique as well and the last two chapters were critiques of the work by an interloper, deliberately done to add to the effect. The last chapter or epilogue or 'my thesis proper' titled *'Om Gurubraham Mamamyham!'* continues the language debate. The reviewer says he writes in Indian-English in defence of the author and in keeping with the comic nature of the book points out wrong usages:

Myself having been brought up on the classics the Authorised Version and the Bard, I may submit to you Mr H. Hatterr, that your prose composition is unacceptable. The scenario, laissez-aller is full of serious mistakes. Least to say, an author has no right to do so. An English author must learn to write the English language, please. Why do you not write a simple, concise, straight phrase like *To be or not to be* which has all the virtues of prose composition, rhetoric, style etc and no ambiguity whatever, being Anglo-Saxon assonance and no Romance as the highest English composition should be? Why do you repeat yourself, excuse me? Why do your write such difficult English language for the literati...?

In terms of writing a novel in Indian-English, Hatterr's successor arrived only six decades later in 1991, when Delhi-based Anurag Mathur wrote *The Inscrutable Americans*. This unassuming, unpretentious novel went straight to the heart of the Indian reader and it has become perhaps the largest selling original title published in India, with thirty-four editions till 2005. Now, of course, some of Chetan Bhagat's novels may outsell Mathur's classic. Mathur sent an Indian inadequately armed with English vocabulary to the US for higher education, the very opposite of Desani, who sent Hatterr to India. Both authors seemed to be bent on giving play to Indian-English. Hatterr was partly Indian, but Gopal so homebred. Mathur's dehat-to-disco ride is full of passages of write, in Indian-English! Gopal was living the Great Indian Dream of getting a study visa to the US. Gopal's was the underachieving Indian's leap for the kill. His situation and aspirations and his English were the average Indian's, starry-eyed and lock-jawed at the America that unpeeled in front of him. Gopal, like other users of Indian-English, did not lack bravado in using the language. The letter which begins the novel sets the tone for the comic plight of the narrator as well his pathetic English. In writing his first letter home, he forsakes Hindi with the unquestioned and guiltless ease of all Indians, giving yet another indication of how tenuous the Indian's link with his mother tongue is. The underlying belief is that with Hindi as your metier you cannot achieve much.

> Beloved younger Brother,
> Greetings to Respectful parents. I am hoping all is well with health and wealth. I am fine at my end. Hoping your end is fine too. With God's grace and parents' Blessings I am arriving safely in America and finding good apartment near University. Kindly assure mother that I am strictly consuming vegetarian food only in restaurants though I am not knowing cooks are Brahmins. I am also constantly remembering Dr Verma's advice and strictly avoiding American women and other unhealthy habits. I hope Parent's Prayers are residing with me.
>   Younger Brother I am having so many things to tell you I am not knowing where to start. Most surprising thing about America is it is full of Americans. Everywhere Americans, Americans, Americans big and white it is little frightening. The flight from New Delhi to New York is arriving safely thanks to God's Grace and Parents Prayers and mine too. I am not able to go to bathroom whole time because I am sitting in corner seat as per revered Grandmother's wish. Father is rightly scolding that airplane is flying too high good view. Still please tell her I have done needful...
> Gopal

From a blog, written one guesses by a bright Bengali author whose debut novel was not picked up by UK publishers, comes this wonderful satire on this Indian-writing-in-English tamasha and the review cottage industry that has sprouted around it. There are wonderful touches and swipes at the paraphernalia surrounding Indian writing in English, an honour not given to other Indian languages in which stories are being told every day. There has been a spurt in publicity on the subject of late, with TV channels taking due interest in Indian-English and a few filmmakers making an entry into this theatre of so much *halla gulla,* flanked by outriders and kettle-drummers. The verse in Indian-English is original stuff, so is the name of the blog: Putu the Cat.

Putu's Literary Saga with Happy Ending
Dedicated to Tiger of Bengal, Pride of Nation, nephew of Putu.

Putu writing classic book
Gentle reader, come take look
Putu's magic pen on thaba
Putu will be Rushdie's baba

Putu finish classic novel
Agent publisher all grovel
Banging door of Putu's house
Running like the three blind mouse

Putu is craze song and dance
Has mosto foreign advance
Putu is sure shot for Booker
All say Putu sexy looker

All reviewer, one by one
Saying Putu son of gun
Mixing Dan Brown mass appeal
With G. Marquez magic real

NDTV girl with paunch
Asking quote at launch

Asking Putu, tell the nation
What is Putu's inspiration?

Putu says, dear girl, as such
None is fix but ilish maach
Sometimes little mangsho bhaat
Quicking beat of Putu's heart

That is all Putu is needing
Thank you for coming to reading
NDTV lady smile
Charmed is all by Putu style

Vikram, Zadie, VS, Hari
All sitting in Putu's bari
Putu curling lengthy whisker
Drinking Pepsi with Talisker

All say Putu what is next?
What will be next epic text?
Putu saying fiddlesticks
No more verbal gymnastics

Mira Nair came on phone
Would not leave Putu alone
Book shook writing jolly good
But now time for Bollywood

Putu book will now be movie
All will be disco and groovy
Besides writer Putu'll be
Idol, Bombay matinee

With Putu as leading star
Music mix by Bappi da
With Shah Rukh as villain plumber

Yana Gupta item number

So when you see Putu Cat
Become great aristocrat
Wearing coat with skin of dog
Remember this Putu blog

But who can forget Allan Sealy, whose mock-epic *Trotter-Nama* took us into the Anglo-Indian world? 'All Anglos were writers until the railways came, almost all. Soldiers and teachers too—we're still that though there aren't many of us left. Maybe a hundred thousand, maybe two, counting the bazaar-side Anglos.'

We had to wait a long time after Rushdie for another landmark Indian novel to come our way. Arundhati Roy had given inklings of her immense talent by scripting, participating and acting in 'lunatic fringe films', but nothing, nothing at all prepared us for *The God of Small Things*. In its inventiveness, the sheer audacity of the way it handled language, its sarcasm, the high realm it reached and occupied, every which way we look at it, it dazzled, it enlightened, it provoked, it made us laugh out loud. For all that, *Small Things* is nothing short of a classic.

English or Indian writing in English was to be taken further from where Rushdie left it. Many passages in GOST had the earthiness which only Indian languages can have. The regional and the universal concerns segued so seamlessly in the book that we are filled with a sense of wonder. I read the book once again, ten years after I first read it in manuscript form. My copy had an inscription in it by Arundhati, 'For Binoo and Rebecca—Binoo the first person in the World to review my book!' A tinge of leg-pulling there, I guess, but I had treasured the copy and it was not until ten years later that I could go back to it.

The book and two articles I had written about it haunted me. Many years after I wrote the cover story for *India Today* on her Booker Prize, people to whom I was introduced suddenly sprang up and greeted me with warm handshakes. As I looked puzzled, they would explain how they liked this particular article. Later I realized that many people who talked authoritatively about COST hadn't read the book, especially in literate Kerala where no book priced at above ₹50 is bought but still is discussed threadbare. So they had enough reason to be thankful to me for giving them a glimpse into Papachi's world. Much to my utter surprise and delight, the piece found its way into 'Best of 30 years of *India Today*'. Which sparked off another series of handshakes and 'Oh, yes you wrote that piece-type-of-thing'. The speakers in such cases continued to inform me all about Roy: 'Delhi girl—rebel girl—beautiful girl in beautiful house girl—like mother like daughter, you know, no?—you've met her, ohh?—you've seen her, ohhh?—your first read her copy, ohhhh?—it is post modernist no doubt at all—aiyoo waat a book—simmply wat nolege about English, she has, no, and without any nolege degree in English, no?'

Finally, I got down to read it for the second time after the long 1997-2006 gap. I had grown, I had aged, levels of cynicism in me had risen. I feared I would hate the book this time. Fortunately, I didn't, but like with all books that have the grade of timelessness pasted on it the book had shifted with a tectonic heave to place itself in new circumstances and times.

The novel is throughout a confrontation with English. It is a confrontation in which the author wins all the time and the language too gains. 'Win-win situation' as headlines say. Early on in the novel, Aunt Baby Kochamma punishes the twins for daring to speak in Malayalam, just as their mother Ammu tries to further their interest in English.

That whole week Baby Kochamma eavesdropped relentlessly on the twins' private conversation and whenever she caught them speaking in Malayalam, she levied a small fine which was deducted at source. From their pocket money. She made them write lines—'impositions' she called them *I will always speak in English. I will always speak in English.* A hundred times each. When they were done she scored them out with her red pen to make sure that old lines were not recycled for new punishments...

This is a punishment which generations of urban middle-class children in India had to face. This relentless purging of the mother tongue from the minds of children is a continuing process done under the supervision of urban uppity mothers and nosey aunts and mothers-in-law like Baby Kochamma, who is actually a pan-Indian caricature. In innocent Indian minds, English almost always starts as punishment, as an imposition. For me too—I learnt to spell this way. From these painful beginnings, English then takes over the lives of people, like it did in the case of Arundhati. Or in the case of many English writers and journalists who keep afloat a variety of English publications, from dailies to weeklies, to brochures masquerading as magazines, magazines pretending to be brochures, publications appropriated by the Right, weeklies propounding Leftist theories—a menagerie of English that helps further India's relationship with the language and, in the process, contributes cliches, Indianisms and Hinglish which make the language vaguely comprehensible even to non-speakers.

The Indian way of writing English, the same intuitions that lead hoarding painters to resort to their own spellings and grammar can be seen in Estha's story, called 'Little Ammu', about his mother. Such childish misspelling is the staple of the user of

Indian-English. Elements of childishness carried into adulthood is one of the drivers of Indian-English. This is not to suggest that users of Indian-English have a stunted mental growth. But in terms of vocabulary, yeah:

> On Saturday we went to a bookshop in Kottayam to buy Ammu a present because her birthday is in 17th of novembre. We bote her a diary. We hid it in the coberd and then it began to be night. Then we said do you want to see your present and she said yes I would like to see it and we wrote on the paper For a Little Ammu with Love from Estha and Rahel and we gave it to Ammu and she said what a lovely present its jut what I whanted and then we talked for a little while and we talked about the diary and then we gave her a kiss and went to bed.

They went to bed in the daytime too. For an 'afternoon gnap'. The afternoon nap has caused problems not just for Rahel. Maybe it's a Kottayam thing, since a snore in the afternoon after a heavy multi-curry meal ringed with fish and *thorans* (any vegetarian preparation sprinkled with coconut) is a must. 'Meals ready. Curd extra. Rice any amount No prablem' is such an enticing announcement for any Keralite as he travels up and down his country in search of the God (Marxist, reformist or just remittance) that owns the place.

A professor of English in a college next to where the Meenachal flows once told me, 'I will just be back after an afternoon snap. *Oru cheirya* snap, just a small snap.'

'Which studio?' I asked.

Even the scatology in GOST is enticing and riveting. Accomplished by sometimes resorting to nonsense verse in an English so familiar in 'English-medium' schools across the country:

Hey Mr Monkey Man
Why's your BUM so Red?
I went for SHIT to Madras
And scraped it till it Bled!

Apart from anything else that the novel offered, Indian-Englishness that is caricatured and satirized goes straight to the heart of the Indian reader. His guilt at not being able to master the language, his 'various troubles' with the language are all taken care of in this book. The guilt has been washed clean. At last, he can have fun with English.

9

'TELL ME SOMETHING, *MERI JAAN*'

Come and meet me at the backside
—Lady teacher to hero in *Main Hoon Na*

Users of English have often been objects of ridicule, hatred, jealousy and admiration. They are remnants or by-products of the Raj, their intentions are suspect, they are possible inheritors of wealth and social status, they speak in a tongue which makes little sense to the hardcore desi Indian. Perfect to be mocked at. Over the years, Hindi cinema did it with tremendous effect, bringing roars of laughter from the front-benchers to the balcony—and now the premium lounges of multiplexes.

The caricatured Angreziwallah always appealed to the front-bencher, going by the success of such movies. He was pictured invariably with suspenders holding up pants wound around a bulging waistline. Sometimes he came with a top hat too, as Amitabh Bachchan did, prancing around as Antony Gonsalvez, using rhyming English words. The heroine in such set scenes mostly wore a frock, had heavyweight boobs and heavy lips and thick lip-gloss, shimmying up the image of the Indian foreigner. These set pieces helped the director stage ballroom dances with a grand piano and extras lined up watching the show. These have mostly gone out of fashion now. But in those days it let the hero lift the lady up and swing her around as the audience gaped at her legs and hoped they could get to see a flash of her underwear—which never happened on the Indian screen, despite many heroines coming perilously close to letting millions have a peek. Lately, some heroines have crossed barriers, but it can't be said they learnt anything from their Hollywood counterparts.

Such peek-a-boo voyeurism was denied, but there were other pleasures and laughs in store all the time. English provided the logic and the lines. In a modern, disturbing and mostly English-Hindi movie, *Being Cyrus,* the police officer brilliantly played by Manoj Pahwa chats up the lady about his job and says how he has had a 'shoulder disallocation' beating up some guys. Bits and pieces of such lines were enough, and everything worked.

Like the police officer, everyone now uses Indian-English, not just the Parsi (though *Being Cyrus* is a Parsi film). The mechanic, the gangster, the sidekick—they all deliver punchlines in English. Derek Bose, Bollywood watcher and author of *Everybody Wants a Hit,* says, 'Till the mid-eighties, Goan Christian and Parsi characters had to speak Bombaiya *maka-pao* English. Today everybody is speaking English. From the ex-Army man to the mechanic to the convent-educated girl to the nurses to foreign-returned NRIs. That cliche no doubt exists, but it is less pronounced, probably because of the type of films being made.'

Hindi jokes work too, but Indian-English characters are good subjects for caricature and in the process raise quite a few laughs.

Here too the Indian who speaks English in a Hindi movie and the Tom Alter-type Raj remnant speaking English should be viewed differently. English as an instrument of parody is a common feature. Occasionally, English is used to give a fillip to set pieces like disco scenes. Many songs with English lines have gone on to become pan-Indian hits, like 'Just chill', chanted over and over again, and 'Tell me something, *meri jaan*' in mock-rap numbers. The soul has gone out of lyrics and in its place come Indianized versions of hip-hop and rap and all that. People who hum these songs in the seething Indian suburbia and mohallas do not bother about the meaning or the context. They are songs from Hindi movies sung by their favourite heroes and heroines and that is what matters. For them, 'Just chill' would just mean that the hero is recommending chilled beer—or 'Child BeAr' as it is advertised in many grog shops in the Hindi heartland. Also, film makers realize that Indian-English rip-offs work more than actual English dialogues. It is because the masses, the front-benchers, who make or break a movie, use them too, and it goes straight to their hearts.

Nothing worked like the Ajit jokes. A villain who acted in over 100 films, Ajit, or Hamid Ali Khan, who died on 22 October 1998, was the archetypal villain if ever there were one. The masses loved him because he played the villain the way a villain was perceived to be. He had a moll, Mona darling, by his side. In *Zanjeer,* he told her, 'Lily, don't be silly'—four simple words which are chanted till today and everywhere raise a few smirks and laughs, recalling the great Indian villain who wore dark glasses, chomped on a cigar, had a sidekick called Raabert (Robert), spoke in Indian-English and issued threats. Those who wrote out his scripts, like Salim and Javcd, had the pulse of the masses. Once Ajit asked them if anyone of them had seen an angry gangster and Salim said they only saw smiling gangsters like Haji Mastan and the phenomenally famous Varadarajan, both of whom inspired movies and characters. So Ajit became the smiling gangster (a character improved upon in later movies) He called himself 'loin' in *Kallicharan* and not 'lion', just the way many Punjabis referred to the majestic animal. To refer to loin was to immediately recall the villain and at the same time summon up Indian-English jokes. Ajit had the great Indian aspiration rolled into him—the moll, the sidekick and the English—and it suited everyone fine.

He referred to his moll as 'Mona darling', and that too became a pan-Indian favourite. 'He always used to tell me that he loved the dialogue beginning with "Mona darling...." In his opinion it was one of the best dialogues in his films,' producer Prakash Mehra was to say after Ajit died. The 'loin' and 'Mona darling' jokes with their bilingual puns were to become phrases of common usage in India. Regional films tried their best to redo the Ajit act with partial success.

Among dumb blondes, Mona will rank quite highly considering that she refuses to die, just like her master Ajit. The boss once wanted to cut off her hands because: 'Typing *nahin aati hat. Kamsekam* shorthand *seekhna chahiye.*' Shakespeare too came into Ajit's repertoire: '*Inko* Hamlet poison *khilado,*' Ajit tells Raabert. '*Sochta rahega* to be or not to be.'

It is through Ajit jokes, created long after he died, that we realize how much English—or the Indian version of English—could appeal to a larger audience to which the language is otherwise not accessible. English thus exists as a backdrop in a million minds. For many, it is a dolled-up poster announcing your aspirations. You are unwilling or unable to use it unless provoked by Ajit or Amitabh Bachchan. Then this unused lingua franca assumes a life all its own. This language has no hope of making it mainstream. But it is there to delight everyone at the right time. Bollywood English is a caricature, a presumed language of an Indian videshi class, and so the language becomes the main tool, quite an effective one at that.

English was used to bridge the divide between the aspiring Indian and the 'BPL (below poverty line) types'—the real Indian for whom the Hindi movie is actually made. They are the most vulnerable, easily won over; they like the outrageous songs and they suspend disbelief easily. So cerebral directors who tried to reflect inner pain and inner journeys saw their art-house efforts crash. Reality was too difficult to digest. Bring on the song and the dance and the love requited in the foothills of the Himalayas.

So Amitabh Bachchan (who else?) it was who did one of the most memorable Indian-English takes we have seen in Bollywood. In *Namak Halaal*, he was the native who would confront the aspiring English-speaking 'other India' on his own terms, in his own English. He suddenly finds himself in front of a manager as a job applicant. Faced with the prospect of having to speak English, like millions of Indians every day, Bachchan launches forth into a mock cricket commentary, which is again the average Indian's first introduction to English. Amitabh goes on a nonstop commentary about something happening between Vijay Merchant and Vijay Hazare. It is alliterative and rhyming as well. He, of course, lands a job as a waiter.

Just before he had to prove his English credentials, Bachchan had played the perfect rustic who finds himself in a party full of whisky glasses, pearl necklaces, cleavages, fat thighs, glittering see-through costumes (which, alas, never gives a glimpse of the nipple, despite promising so much). Perfect setting for a dance scene—and Bachchan, who had played the ass perfectly, diving here and there trying to fish out his slipper which had fallen into the pool in the atrium, sings a song in true folk style.

This constant confrontation of rustic and sophisticate has provided Hindi cinema with regular laugh scenes, apart from some splendid songs. Songs had anyway often resorted to exhortation and romantic pleadings in English. When the hero realized that using the word 'mohabbat' as an offering of love may not work, he always switched to English and told her, 'Julieeee, I love you.' These English entreaties seemed to have a better effect both on the heroine and the audience. So lyricists from the 1960s down to the irreverent writers of the present day resorted to love messages in Indian-English.

There are various such professions of love. 'I love you, Sayyoni', like Himesh Reshammiya sang, is one of the most used direct no-frills opening lines. If the hero realizes that he has not made much headway, he normally sings, 'Love will find a way, Jaaniye'. Of course it will. And so will Indian-English. The popularity of rock music and item numbers in discos put the Hindi film songwriter in a bit of a fix. The locale had changed from the municipal park in the corner of town to the hitherto unimaginable undulating landscape of Europe with the Alps, tulips and the slow-moving tram as backdrop. There was no point taking the lead pair all the way to the shadow of the Alps and making him confess his 'mohabbat' to his heroine. The back-up team was also full of foreign dancers and they did not know how to act coy and then glance at the hero fleetingly, with the sari covering the head.

The lyricist had to come up with some lingo that would win the heart of a paan-chewing front-bencher as well as a post-millennium, multi-tasking Indian babe who loves to flaunt her bra strap, uses Bluetooth and pouts a pierced lip.

So the lyricist of Karan Johar's *Kabhi Alvida Na Kehna* came up with this mongrel song: 'Where's the Party Tonight?'

Nach all night
Wanna *nach* all night
Do you feel alright
Wanna *nach* all night
Dance with me baby
Won't you dance with me all night?
Won't you party party party
Won't you burn the floor all night

Pyaare pyaare lamhe
Pyaari pyaari baaten
Sapnon ke din hain
Sapnon ki raaten
Goonje hain dil ke taraney
Machle hain geet suhaane
Behke hain saare deewane
Toh nachle nachle all night

Where's the party tonight?
(Somewhere all night)
Where's the party tonight
(On the dance floor)
Sapnon ke din hain
Sapnon ki raaten
Where's the party tonight…

It doesn't matter that there is often a disconnect between the song and the movie. Under the all-embracing term 'item number', the digressions into another terrain, the forays into raunchiness, the taunting tonality of the songs, the rhyming patterns that would make even a country bumpkin do a jig—all this allowed a familiarity with Indian-English to be displayed. The forest or fountain or the park was not usually where the English was tried out. The disco was always there and if not there could always be the party where Indian Made Foreign Liquor (IMFL) was served. Indian Made English Language (IMEL) was the right choice too. So 'rock and roll, baby', 'you are my love', 'dance with me, baby' and 'I wanna go dancing' were all unquestioningly accepted. These lines did not mock at the non-English speaker. They were all reminders to the public that another language was at their door and they better start swaying to its tune.

In its blind imitation of lines from Western rock and rap, Hindi is unapologetic. Bollywood is all-conquering and a good part of its viewership is abroad. So the director and the songwriter now have to cast their net wider. The non-resident Indian would love dances in the disco. He would love the imitation of rap numbers. Bhangra-rap has already made its presence felt, and the large number of Punjabi viewers in the US and UK took all this as a tribute to their growing influence in determining the content of Bollywood films. In all this, English lines played a part.

The English does not easily segue into the Hindi lines, as we see in the party number. But who cares? The English makes known the movie's ambition, and the front-bencher gets the chance to see a sexy number—cleavage, legs, and all that. He does not complain. So when the lady sings, 'Let's party tonight', none of them think the film is going to take a political turn and a new party going to be launched to counter the Samajwadi Party in Uttar Pradesh.

10

EPISTOLARY EPILOGUE

*In which the immortal
reader-cum-writer gives it those ones*

Shri Readerji,
   All this you read and lauf. Why lauf? Our English language experience come from Speedex yes and it serves all our purposes like last week I write love letter with emotion and heart to a girl in post office rumbala district jagdevpur. I do inauguration for that letter with line from new Speedex English-Hindi-Urdu-English (complete in 30 days or money return) on page 242 which is a good for romanticism: 'Dear my pussycat, Your face are fresh as the daisy flowers and your lips is waiting for my imprinting of myself on yourself which I hope to do soon without parental people standing nearby.' So my English language experience will score victory over her heart and then we will both go to abroad countries for our MA (Cam).

   But now I come to hear from my many of my co-brothern

in the rajdhani city of New Dilli that blasted place, that lot off matters have been written by one nonsense person about Indian-English to be made into a book. This rajdhani is full of ultrasound in the roads I cannot hear when I come here so big is the traffics. That is why I go to small town Meerut becase in rajdhani I get labour pain when I think of working because I cannot work at all so hot and so cold. So I decide not to be disallocated from Meerut.

But why? Why always make fun of we Indian people who studied in government secondary school, district Meerut?

In all my letters to *Bihar Herald* newspaper from times immemorial, I have been a regular watcher of all the sentences manufactured by the colony peoples and the Indian peoples after 1947 was obtained without much bloody fighting. That Gandhi write in English and wear dress in dehati style like many Biharis and nicely the Englishman call him naked fakir which is the nice word for religious peoples near temples.

Now there is new book on Indian peoples who make their own words in English and trying to be sahib. We the real people of maha bharat are always being painted with the phoren toothbrush. Such people want to make fun at us and that is why this new book. Our English is superior English and we know that the big dictionaries like Rapidex and Oxford books take many words from us and so give us the big outstanding ovation. But Indian people don't like us at all never, never. There is one man I know who do articles in the Dehli papers about the mistakings people like me and others from Hindi places do in English. That is not our problem you know. Our English speakings is better than all the useless nonsense things that come in nowadays papers which have only Indian womans in nudity poses exposing their pleasure parts to all peoples like that Shrawat girl who is jat girl with Amrican facelook, Hollywood brestlook. Like Sardarjis we never look at backsides of womans but these papers all give such too many clickings of bottomsides.

But this one man who is a gujju bhai but says only English language is a fun-maker of all of us from Meerut and neighbouring parts of UP-Bihar. Why he not know guju language? He make all mistake in Guju langege is it not?. I know all these type of peoples who say they are Gujju and talk only in whiteman language. He make fun always with us people who are born in dehati places. I am so angry with the many articles about original Bharat English and my finger is typing badly in this compooter in the Chit-Chat cyber cafe (₹15 only for one hours) in this Malilapur near eastern UP.

How when we all from Bharat and yet they call it Indian-English. Yes now I remember his name which is called Jack Soorya and he make all of India laugh at us. He always write one day that 'don't take your grandfather's time to do your homework' which I hear first time only. Then he also said that 'I will make you remember your nani' which the once-alive Rajiv Gandhi our dear Prime minister said from Ram Leela ground to encourage the fear in BJP party. That man think he make fun of us and get some sabhahshi from his malik and no retirement for many many years even after he attain superannuality. He know only Englishs of rich patelbhais and what he know about english of sardarji and all the rich panjabis who go to place called New yark and drive the taxi and also some sardarjis go to Caliphornia and Canda and do all the agricultural businesss which is full of apples which come to us with small sticker sticking on red apples which is like painted apple and we pay more money for one pav of that apple instead of our Kashmiri apple.

They all speak in amrikan English and are very rich and get richer while patelbhais like Jack know only guju english. All nonsense and no full stop to the funny words. This letter I am writing to the Dehli paper because I read the paper for long time before I see the pleasure parts of all the capital womans and they are also drinking wisky in glass with cigarette in the finger and showing some jewels put inside of the small gole of the stomak and some of them show the secret wearings and chaddis inside the jene pants.

Now again there is big book on the language of the poor people of bharat. Real India is in the village you know no? This book also by some very unfamous writer also simply make fun of our English. Why? Why no fun of Amrickan language which we see in the movies. Why? Why no fun of bad language used by all the good people who say bloody and bastard always at all times even in the compooter cafe and Udipi cafe? Who know that oxford and Cambrij also accept our language and many of our people are doing big degrees in those places and come back with gora womans. Will these womans come with our boys if he don't know the good English. Why? You answer now to me ok? Then we talk about the great mistakes in this unfamous writers' book. Every man is trying to repeat the nonsens of this Soorya man and we will take all this to the legal brains and get our instant remedies, for the label cases.

The new book I know will be all bakwas stuff about we people. The hazaar fundas of Indian English is what? All galath and mistakings. There is vas deferens between funny and serious and how to write a book on the English we all talk so nicely. It is our history when we throw out the colny people of East Indian company. We did not talk the language of the goras and we talk of only our language and so they got defeated. Not Gandhi who write in English and talk of our Hindi problems. Language is our own from the earth and mud of our land which we agriculture the bhindi. Bharat zindabad. After writing this long letter my heart is fulfilled with happy and joy since I reply well to all those unfamous writer who make fun of us. Any such book we will light fire like the Ravan and send it like cracker rocket.

Dear editorji when you print this letter in the pages of your newspaper please send me two copies by registered post to the aforementioned male address pronto.

Wishes to all the nears and dears.

Mr Prasad Antony Ja (BA-Pat)
Proprietor: Famous Tailoring (Global famous for soots and pants for marriage parties)

SELECT BIBLIOGRAPHY

Aitchison, C. U. (comp.), *A collection of treaties, engagements relating to India and neighbouring countries*, Government Printing Press, 1909.

Anglo-Indian Domestic Life—A Letter from an Artist in India to His Mother in English, Thacker, Spink and Co., London, 1862.

Buchanan, Francis, *An Account of the District of Bhagalpur in 1810-11*, Patna Law Press.

Carmichael, Amy Wilson, *Things As They Are; Mission Work in Southern India*, Kerwick Missionary, Morgan and Scott, London.

Crawford, John, *Letters from British Settlers in the Interior of India*, 1831.

Forrest, George W. (ed.), Selections from the letters, dispatches and other state papers preserved in the Bombay Secretariat, Vol. 1, Government Central Press, Mumbai, 1887.

Foster, William (ed.), *Letters Received by the East India Company from Its Servants in the East, Vol. III, 1615*, Sampson Low Marston and Company, Fleet Street, London, 1899.

Khair, Tabish, *Alienation in Contemporary Indian English Novels*, OUP, New Delhi, 2001.

Lamba, C. P., *Thoughts and Reflections*, Chandra Mohan Lamba, Allahabad.

Mehrotra, A. K. (ed.), *The Illustrated History of Indian Writing in English*, Permanent Black, New Delhi, 2003.

Nair, P. Thankappan, *Hicky and His Gazette*, S and T Book Stall, Kolkata.

Nair, P. Thankappan, *Proceedings of the Asiatic Society, 1833-1841, Vol. IV.*

Nehra, Arvind, *Letters of an Indian Judge to an English Gentlewoman*, Peter Davies Ltd, 1934.

Oaten, Edward Farley, *European Travellers in India*, Kegan Paul Trench Trubner and Company.

Ravoof, A. A., *Nehru: The Man*, Pearl Publications, Mumbai.

Taraporewala, Jehangir Sorabji, *Elements of the Science of Language*, Calcutta University, 1978, first edition October 1931.

Toller, T. N., *Outlines of the History of the English Language*, University Press, Cambridge, 1900.

Vazeeruddin, Mohd, *Nonsense Essays*, Literature House, Amritsar.

Whitworth, George Clifford, *Indian English: An Examination of the Errors of Idiom made by Indians in Writing English*, Garden City Press, Danvers, 1907.

Others

A collection of the Acts passed by the Governor General of India in Council in 1921.

Translation of the new Kowlnama or Agreement given by the Nawab-ud Dowla to Rajah Cheyl Singh, 6 September 1773.